D0762009

THE
PROFANE
ART

Essays and Reviews

THE PROFANE ART

Essays and Reviews

Joyce Carol Oates

E. P. DUTTON, INC.   NEW YORK

"Imaginary Cities: America" was commissioned by the Conference on Literature and the Urban Experience, Rutgers University at Newark, April 17–20, 1980.

"At Least I Have Made a Woman of Her" was commissioned by the Conference on Changing Perspectives on Intimacy, Sexuality, and Commitment, at the University of Hartford, June 7–18, 1982, and will appear in *The Georgia Review,* Spring 1983.

"The Magnanimity of *Wuthering Heights*" appeared in *Critical Inquiry,* Winter 1983.

"Charles Dodgson's Golden Hours" appeared in *Soaring with the Dodo: Essays on Lewis Carroll's Life and Art,* Edward Guiliano and James R. Kincaid, eds. Charlottesville: LCSNA and the Univ. Press of Virginia, 1982; and *English Language Notes,* 20, No. 2 (December 1982), 109–118.

"John Updike's American Comedies" appeared, in somewhat different form, in *Modern Fiction Studies,* Fall 1975.

"Notes on Failure" appeared in *Hudson Review,* Summer 1982.

"The Interior Castle: The Art of Jean Stafford's Short Fiction" appeared in *Shenandoah* XXX, No. 3, Winter 1979.

"Colette's Purgatory," "Géza Csáth's Garden," "The 'Mysticism' of Simone Weil," "Legendary Jung," "Sacred and Profane Iris Murdoch" appeared in *The New Republic,* often in somewhat different forms.

"Before God was Love: The Short Stories of Paul Bowles," and "Anne Sexton: Self-Portrait in Poetry and Letters" appeared in the *New York Times Book Review*.

Published in the United States by E. P. Dutton, Inc.,
2 Park Avenue, New York, N.Y. 10016

Library of Congress Cataloging in Publication Data
Oates, Joyce Carol,
   The profane art.
   1. Literature, Modern—History and criticism—Addresses, essays, lectures. I. Title.
PN710.19
1983   809'.03   82-14769

ISBN: 0-525-24166-3

Published simultaneously in Canada by Clarke, Irwin & Company Limited, Toronto and Vancouver

10 9 8 7 6 5 4 3 2 1

First Edition

For Karen Braziller

Contents

REVIEWS

THE PROFANE ART

Essays and Reviews

Introduction

The motives for criticism are even more puzzling than the motives for art. The systematic reflection upon another's creativity; the exploration of the subtleties of a work that lie, in a sense, mute within it; the dialogue with an invisible and perhaps skeptical audience asserting that a work is more resourceful, more astonishing than a casual reading can suggest—all contribute to the critical impulse.

Criticism speaks, as Northrop Frye has observed—and all the arts are silent. Their expression is only *of* themselves and never *for* themselves.

Medusa, that terrible image-bearing goddess of Greek mythology, could not be encountered directly by the hero Perseus, for her power was such that she turned all who gazed upon her into stone. (The "Gorgon" Medusa, formerly a beautiful woman, had been transformed into a winged monster with glaring eyes, tusklike teeth, claws, and—most famously—serpents in place of hair.) Only through indirection, by means of a polished shield, could she be approached in order to be slain. One cannot resist reading the tale as a cautionary parable: the inchoate and undetermined event, the act without structure, without the necessary confinement of the human imagination, is simply too brutal—because too inhuman—to be borne. Perseus, aided by Athene, conquers the barbaric in nature (in his own nature?) by means of reflection. The demonic Medusa is successfully subdued by the godly strategy of restraint, confinement, indirection—in short, by a kind of art; an artfulness that substitutes intellectual caution for the brashness of primitive instinct. So art labors to give meaning to a profusion of meanings; its structures—inevitably "exclusive"—provide a way of seeing with the mind's eye. The journalist's or the historian's hope of gathering in all truths is surrendered in the interest of exploring a single truth. The restraint of art—its subjectivity, its stubborn faith in its own music, an angle of vision, an overriding emotion, an obsession—is its power.

Criticism is, then, the art of reflection upon reflection. It is a distinctly and wonderfully *civilized* venture: the unhurried, systematic, discursive commentary upon another's vision. Its impulses are to synthesize, to abbreviate, to exclaim over origins, analogues, hidden meanings. Like gems turned slowly in the hand, diffracting light in new and startling patterns, all serious works of art yield a multiplicity of meanings. The critic's reflective activity is altogether natural—which is to say "instinctive" and "real"—but this is a naturalness that finds its most comfortable expression in the scrutiny of the artist's interpretation of an image. Not Medusa herself, with her galaxy of possible meanings, but the highly polished shield in which she is framed: the *art* of the shield, in fact; the stratagems of Perseus who is human, and consequently the real object of our fascinated interest. If the greatest works of art sometimes strike us as austere and timeless, self-contained and self-referential, with their own private music, as befits sacred things, criticism is always an entirely human dialogue, a conversation directed toward an audience. It is a conversation between equals, on a subject of acknowledged superiority. Which is why, for many of us, reading it and writing it are such extraordinarily rewarding activities. There is a profoundly satisfying beauty in the very gesture of acquiescence to another's vision—the communal acknowledgment of the greatness and abiding worth of certain works of art. These are, of course, our "sacred things."

Auden has said, "The value of a profane thing lies in what it usefully does, the value of a sacred thing lies in what it *is*." Of course the "sacred thing" may also have a function but that is not its primary role. If art is sacred it is quite reasonable to assume that criticism is profane: it exists not in and for itself; it justifies itself as a service. The artist participates in a sacred rite, the critic in a profane rite. Yet are the two inevitably opposed? Must they be adversaries? There is a chilling truth to Nietzsche's characteristically terse observation that praise is more obtrusive than blame, but both praise and blame are perhaps beside the point in a systematic and reflective criticism. The secular nature of the critical enterprise, its willingness to be second-ary, in the service of, *profane* in Auden's sense of the word, gives it a freedom not always available to the artist himself.

Yet there is a tradition of criticism as warfare, defensive or otherwise. The rationalist and combative approach, in which works of art are on trial, to be judged by the critic, insists upon the critics's strength and the artist's passivity. The one represents reason (in its most sinister guise it is presented as "common sense"), the other represents passion, disorder, instability, even madness. Nearly all critics are conservative if only because they cannot presume to judge art by its own standards if those standards are new: even the most well-intentioned critic carries about with him, unacknowledged, his ideas of what a *novel* or a *short story* or a *play* or a *poem* should be, based upon works he has studied. His instinct is to preserve the past because it is *his* past; he has a great deal invested in it. The artist, by contrast, really must follow his instinct into areas not yet mined by others—he cannot even console himself (unless he is Joyce or Stendhal or Flaubert, with a prodigious faith in his own genius) that criticism will someday "catch up" with his innovations. What appears as disorder, instability, and frequent madness to the critic is in fact the creative activity itself: it seeks to blossom in inhospitable climates, break free of its confining species, celebrate the individual and the idiosyncratic, even at the cost of official—that is, "critical"—censure. So it is commonplace to read of the dismaying critical receptions given great works of art, and it is never surprising to discover, in perusing the past, that the best-received works, the *really* successful works, are often by people whose names have long been forgotten.

The history of the critic's distrust of art is hardly felicitous, but it is certainly instructive if one wants to arrive at an understanding of the tacit conservatism of most critics. Consider Plato's *Ion,* for instance, which dramatizes Socrates's surprising hostility toward poets. Why did he so distrust the poetic impulse? Was he not a poet himself? Or was it precisely the poet in himself he feared? Nietzsche has spoken contemptuously of the "Greek superficiality" that sought to supplant an older tragic vision, substituting the bloodless play of logic for the full expression of the emotions, and nowhere is this curious and aggressive hostility more forcefully expressed than in certain of Plato's dialogues. It seems difficult for us to believe, judging Plato by our contemporary standards, as if he *were* a contemporary, that he really believed the poetic impulse was divine, for instance, and *only* divine, and that the poet himself had nothing to do with shaping his art. Yet Socrates speaks clearly: ". . . God takes the mind out of the poets, and uses them as his servants, and so also those who chant oracles, and divine seers; because he wishes us to know that not those we hear, who have no mind in them, are those who say such precious things, but God himself is the speaker, and through them he shows his meaning to us. . . . These beautiful poems are not human, not made by man, but divine and made by God; and the poets are nothing but the gods' interpreters, possessed each by whatever god it may be." *Nothing but*! The murderous sophism, the fallacious logic, that denies individuality to the poet precisely because he *is* a poet, and not (for instance) a blacksmith who follows his predecessors in his trade. One could write a lengthy study of the victimization of both the Poet and Woman, presumed by their judges to embody an impersonal and even supernatural value that neverthe-less makes them unfit for most worldly activities, including that of judging. To be *nothing but* possessed by the divine is close to being nothing, in human terms, at all. And the divine may shade horribly into the demonic if the presiding judges decide to revise their judgments.

For despite Socrates's talk of "beauty" and "divinity" we know that the ideal state—the legendary Republic—will not tolerate the presence of poets. Which is to say, in terms of that society, the presence of freethinking individuals, finally ungovernable by external coercion. Of course they must be exiled, under threat of death. Of course they will be killed. From a certain perspective it appears that the sacred rite in which the poet participates is nothing less than the rite of an ineffable freedom of the imagination—in itself paradigmatic of the highest of human experiences.

The ideal criticism, then, aspires to the art of "disinterested" conversation ("disinterested" in Matthew Arnold's sense of the word), a conversation between equals, systematic, unhurried, "profane," reflective. It must take the artist's freedom seriously—it must resist its own conservative and reductive instincts. If only criticism speaks, and all the arts are silent, it is necessary that it speak with both sympathy and rigor; it cannot take its reflective responsibilities lightly.

ESSAYS

Imaginary Cities: America

If the City is a text, how shall we read it?

The manifold evidence of our American literature of the twentieth century suggests that the City, an archetype of the human imagination that may well have existed for thousands of years, in various manifestations (as the Heavenly City, the Kingdom of the Dead, the City of God, the City of Man, the Cities of the Plains, etc.), has absorbed into itself presumably opposed images of the "sacred" and the "secular." The City of God and the City of Man have conjoined out of psychological necessity in an era of diminished communal religion. A result of this fusion of polar symbols is that the contemporary City, as an expression of human ingenuity and, indeed, a material expression of civilization itself, must always be read as if it were Utopian (that is, "sacred")—and consequently a tragic disappointment, a species of hell. A number of our writers have spoken out boldly about the psychological kinship between the

9

individual and the City, interpreting the fate of one in terms of the influence of the other, which is almost always malefic. Saul Bellow's Charlie Citrine says, in his meditation upon the miserable life and premature death of the poet Von Humboldt Fleisher (whom we may equate fairly precisely with Delmore Schwartz): "Chicago with its gigantesque outer life contained the whole problem of poetry and the inner life in America."[1]*

The more autonomous an archetype in the Unconscious, the greater its numinosity in what we might call, echoing Jung, the collective or mass imagination; the more contradictions it displays in consciousness, the greater the range of emotions it arouses. Like Nature (by which I mean, of course, the *idea* of Nature, in itself an invention of civilization—Nature as the timeless though hardly exact counterpart of the City), this image functions almost exclusively as a symbol: it is the dramatic background against which fictional persons enact their representative struggles with those values the City embodies, which are frequently internalized. In America, emphasis has generally been upon the City as an expression of the marketplace struggle that will yield—*should* yield, this being the New World—individual success in financial and social terms: Utopia may not really exist, but the Utopian dream of salvation is still potent. At one extreme, as depicted in the fiction of late nineteenth- and early twentieth-century writers (among them Stephen Crane, Upton Sinclair, Theodore Dreiser, Anzia Yezierska), the struggle is graphic and literal: the City is a place in which human beings die as a consequence of the unspeakable conditions of slum life and actual mistreatment by employers or by one another. "The things which could not kill you," Anzia Yezierska says in the story "My Last Hollywood Script" (1950), "were the making of you,"[2] but very few people were "made" by the exhausting struggle of daily slum life, of which Yezierska writes so powerfully.

At another extreme, in the fiction of the past several decades, and perhaps most eloquently in that of Saul Bellow, the struggle has

---

*Notes to the Essays begin on page 205.

become internalized, a ceaseless philosophical inquiry. Bellow's masterful novels all address themselves to "the lessons and theories of power" in a great American city. Bellow is obsessed with the riddle of what it means to be an urban man in a secular, mass-market culture that appears to be vertiginously extroverted, without a coherent sense of history or tradition—in which, in fact, "all the ages of history" can be experienced as simultaneous.[3] The industrial landscapes of Detroit evoked in Philip Levine's poetry—notably in *They Feed They Lion* and *1933* (1974)—are glimpsed in fragments but coalesce, in the reader's imagination, to a hellish city, a city "pouring fire." And the citizens of Donald Barthelme's *City Life* suspect (probably with justification) that they are suffering brain damage as a result of thei · polluted environment: ". . . we are locked in the most exquisite mysterious muck. This muck heaves and palpitates. It is multidirectional and has a mayor. To describe it takes many hundreds of thousands of words. Our muck is only a part of a much greater muck—the nation-state—which is itself the creation of that muck of mucks, human consciousness."[4]

WOMEN IN CITIES

"No move in this world without money . . ."
—ANZIA YEZIERSKA
"The Miracle"

Students of American literature are all familiar with the hellish City of late nineteenth- and early twentieth-century literature, powerfully presented by writers like Upton Sinclair (whose equation of Chicago with the "jungle" is still, perhaps, a viable image) and Stephen Crane (whose *Maggie: A Girl of the Streets* is set on the Bowery—in Crane's words "the only interesting place in New York"). In reexamining *Maggie* (1896), one is struck by the reiteration of images and scenes of subhuman violence, and by the young novelist's sardonic, objective tone. The City is a "dark region" of "gruesome doorways" that surrender babies to the street and the gutter. Disheveled women gossip with one another in the street or scream "in frantic quarrels." There are aged withered persons, and ragged children, and derelicts, and pugnacious young men who imagine the world "composed, for the most part, of despicable creatures who were all trying to take advantage" of them. The novel's opening scene depicts a merciless fight between two groups of slum children (Rum Alley versus Devil's Row) while adults look on indifferently or with mild curiosity. Maggie's brother Jimmie is savagely stoned by children with "small convulsed faces" and the grins of "true assassins." There is a brilliant three-page tour de force describing Jimmie's experience, years later, as a truck driver in the city, unfortunately too long to quote in its entirety:

> He invaded the turmoil and tumble of the downtown streets, and learned to breathe maledictory defiance at the police, who occasionally used to climb up, drag him from his perch, and punch him. In the lower part of the city he daily involved himself in hideous tangles. . . . He fell into the habit, when starting on a long journey, of fixing his eye on a high and distant object, commanding his horses to start, and then going into a trance of oblivion. Multitudes of drivers might howl in his rear, and passengers might load him with opprobrium, but he would not awaken until some blue policeman . . . began to seize bridles and beat the soft noses of the responsible horses.
>
> . . . Foot passengers were mere pestering flies with an insane disregard for their legs and his convenience. He could not comprehend their desire to cross the streets. Their madness smote him with eternal amazement.
>
> . . . Yet he achieved a respect for a fire-engine. As one charged toward his truck, he would drive fearfully upon a sidewalk, threatening untold people with annihilation. . . . A fire-truck was enshrined in his heart as an appalling thing that he loved with a distant, dog-like devotion. It had been known to overthrow a street-car. . . . The clang of the gong pierced his breast like the noise of remembered war.[5]

The tone is set, in such garish, outsized images, for the destruction of the innocent "girl of the streets" by less physical but equally malicious social forces. Maggie is "ruined," she has "gone to the devil"—and finally commits suicide by throwing herself in the river.

Theodore Dreiser is a far more meticulous observer of city life than Stephen Crane (who was only twenty-one when he wrote *Maggie*), but in *Sister Carrie* (1900) he could not speak more didactically or explicitly:

> When a girl leaves her home at eighteen, she does one of two things. Either she falls into saving hands and becomes better, or she rapidly assumes the cosmopolitan standard of virtue and becomes worse. Of an intermediate balance, under the circumstances [Chicago, 1889] there is no possibility. The city has its cunning wiles, no less than the infinitely smaller and more human tempter. There are large forces which allure with all the soulfulness of expression possible in the most cultured human. The gleam of a thousand lights is often as effective as the persuasive light in a wooing and fascinating eye. Half the undoing of the unsophisticated and natural mind is accomplished by forces wholly superhuman. A blare of sound, a roar of life, a vast array of human hives, appeal to the astonished senses in equivocal terms. . . . Unrecognized for what they are, their beauty, like music, too often relaxes, then weakens, then perverts the simpler human perceptions.[6]

But Carrie is far more resourceful, and more intelligent, than her creator seems to think; despite the leaden moralizing of his prose he allows his heroine to survive the "ruin" of her innocence, unlike Crane's Maggie. She is even fortunate enough to leave somber Chicago for the far more seductive city of New York where, along Broadway, she observes the "sprinkling of goodness and the heavy percentage of vice" parading in the latest, most costly fashions—and is quite dazzled by this "indescribable atmosphere" which has the power to make her forget the old Carrie, her past, and her obligations. (*Sister Carrie* is, it must be said, not really a naturalistic work at all, despite the fact that it deals with ostensibly naturalistic themes. On the contrary, it is a sort of fairy tale—in relation to which Crane's far cruder *Maggie* is the dark and far more convincing cautionary fable.)

Dreiser's pessimism is strongly and provocatively qualified by what might be called his visionary belief that the City, however immediately corrupting, is nevertheless a symbol of the issuant progress of our species. Beyond the individual Carrie and what she presumably represents, Dreiser sees evidence of growth and evolution, even in a determined cosmos: "Among the forces which sweep and play throughout the universe, untutored man is but a wisp in the wind. Our civilization is still in a middle stage, scarcely beast . . . ; scarcely human. . . . We have the consolation of knowing [however] that evolution is ever in action, that the ideal is a light that cannot fail . . ."[7]—a sentiment that seems but slenderly connected to Carrie's story.

Though nearly unknown at the present time, the novelist and short-story writer Anzia Yezierska (1885–1970) is probably a more realistic portrayer of certain aspects of city life in the early years of the twentieth century than her famous male contemporaries. Her writing is autobiographical and emotional. The City of her fiction—New York's Lower East Side, a Jewish ghetto—is complex and ambiguous, by no means simply a marketplace or jungle in which the individual is suffocated.

Between 1920 and 1932 Yezierska published six books, among them her best-known novel, *Bread Givers*. In fast-moving and relatively unsophisticated prose Yezierska dramatizes the struggle of a strong-willed young woman to free herself of both the immigrant slums of the New World and the religiously enjoined subservience and chatteldom of the Old World. Along with her mother and her sisters she is tyrannized by her father, a completely self-absorbed Talmudic scholar who believes that his family exists only to support him. *Bread Givers* evokes an almost Dickensian sense of oppression and injustice: it is shamelessly melodramatic, and yet thoroughly convincing as a document of Yezierska's own emotional experience as the daughter of an extremely religious man. Its picture of the dailyness of life on the Lower East Side, its presentation of the community of Jewish immigrants, has an authenticity lacking in the fiction of most naturalistic writers because it is imagined, as theirs is not, from the inside. Slum life is "real life" to Yezierska, however difficult; in escaping from it one risks losing the connection with life altogether.

Anzia Yezierska was born in a *shtetl* in Russian Poland and emigrated with her family in the 1890s to the New World—to the crowded Lower East Side of Manhattan. In this "new" world Jewish immigrants tried with varying degrees of success and failure to reconstruct the "old" world, and the harrowing conflict between Yezierska's heroines and their conservatively pious fathers must stand as a paradigm of this larger cultural conflict. The Old World makes its claim in this typical outburst of the father in *Bread Givers:* ". . . My books, my holy books always were, and always will be, the light of the world. You'll see yet how all America will come to my feet to learn."[8] Yezierska observes: "The prayers of his daughters didn't count because God didn't listen to women. Heaven and the next world were only for men. Women could get into heaven because they were wives and daughters of men. Women had no brains for the study of God's Torah, but they could be the servants of men who studied the Torah. . . " Her heroine Sara breaks with her family at the age of seventeen—an extraordinarily courageous act, considering her circumstances, and the fact that she has nowhere to live. Her father is outraged and curses her, but she replies: "My will is as strong as yours. I'm going to live my own life. Nobody can stop me. I'm American!"[9]

Sara is bold and impetuous and, in her desperation, exactly right: if she is to save herself from suffocating in her ghetto-bound family she must become *American*. She understands as a very young child that there is "no move in this world without money" and her reasoning leads her to the conclusion that by studying English in night school she will have the means of freeing herself from poverty. And more: "Only to make myself somebody great—and have them [her family] come begging favors at my feet."[10] If the romantically American rags-to-riches plot seems excessive to contemporary readers, one should be reminded that Anzia Yezierska underwent approximately the same experience—her writing is autobiographical in outline if not always in detail.

Where Crane, Dreiser, Henry James, and, indeed, most serious writers of the epoch severely criticized the very basis of "Americani-zation" in these terms, Anzia Yezierska takes everything on faith, knowing only that the future—"America"—is infinitely preferable to the past. She is characterized as a pioneer; her heroine Sara exclaims, as a college girl, "Why is it that when a nobody wants to get to be somebody she's got to make herself terribly hard . . . ?"[11] No one has written with more tenderness and authority of the almost physical yearning for *knowledge* a certain kind of young person possesses. (Is this young person inevitably the child of very poor parents? Or is the struggle for education and self-realization simply more vividly itali-cized in a context of poverty?) Sara wants to raise herself, she wants power, she wants—everything. "Like a starved thing in the dark" she reaches out blindly, sometimes confusing her longing with a longing for men, and bringing about humiliation. But in the end she does triumph, like Yezierska, though she realizes that the shadow of the past, her religious heritage and her elderly father's expectations, still exert their pull. "It wasn't just my father," Sara thinks at the novel's conclusion, "but the generations who made my father whose weight was still upon me."

The City is, ironically, a kind of hell—yet the only possible place for the liberation of a certain kind of independent and courageous woman. The relatively egalitarian nature of the bitter struggle for money allows girls like Yezierska's heroines to break away from the world of their fathers, and if their goals, their triumphs—acquiring a teaching certificate, for instance—seem to us modest enough, we must remember out of what stifling poverty, beneath what appalling low ceilings, they were dreamt. To become a schoolteacher *and* to return to one's old neighborhood!—in triumph and yet in a kind of servitude—this is Sara Smolinsky's achievement. Yezierska herself sold a book of short stories, *Hungry Hearts,* to Sam Goldwyn for $10,000, in 1920, and went to work in Hollywood for a while at a salary of $200 a week; there were sensational "rags-to-riches" stories about her in the Sunday papers; her dreams of greatness were almost alarmingly fulfilled. Interestingly enough, however, she found herself cut off from the source of both her fictional material and her

energy—she felt "without a country, without a people." The congestion and poverty of the Lower East Side, the work she had done in
sweatshops and laundries, perhaps even the bitter struggle with her
family itself were so deeply imprinted in this remarkable woman that,
once free of them, she yearned for them again, recognizing in herself
(as Saul Bellow's far more articulate Augie March recognizes in
himself) the need to be opposed, to be in opposition, to suffer
privation, to *struggle*. The City for all its horrors is the very fountain
of emotion: where else can one experience so much, such a cacopho-
nous variety of sensation? And if one has acquired the City's
language—in this case, "American" English—surely this language
has not the power of moving one's soul as Yiddish does? (Yezierska's
prose style reads as if it were translated from Yiddish—hardly as if it
were self-consciously written at all. Her voice fairly springs out at you
from the page.) At the peak of her success Yezierska found herself
unable to write because, in her words, she had gone "too far away
from life" and did not know how to return. One of her heroines
exclaims: "I don't believe that I shall ever write again unless I can get
back to the real life I once lived when I worked in the factory."

Yezierska writes without irony, however; she is never critical of
the lure of "Americanization" itself. And unlike fellow contemporaries—Henry Roth, for instance, whose *Call It Sleep* is of course a
work of far greater psychological subtlety than Yezierska's—she did
not appear to take an interest in the craft of fiction itself, and one
must read her with expectations appropriate to her intention. The
autobiographical energies of a first-person narration (a "confession,"
a "history," a "defense" of one's present self) need not invariably
bring with them a slackening of control, as Bellow's masterpiece *The
Adventures of Augie March* makes clear, but Yezierska is so close to her
material and to her woman protagonists that the ambiguities that
disturb and enrich "serious" fiction are largely missing. Yet Yezierska
is rarely sentimental about the past, and she certainly does not look
back over her shoulder at Europe—the heroine of "The Miracle," an
early story, wants *only* to escape her Polish village and come to live in
America; the heroine of "America and I," exploited by a well-to-do

Jewish family for whom she works, goes to work in a sweatshop and reads American history in order to dedicate herself to the mission of building "a bridge of understanding between the American-born and myself."

The City's gift of anonymity, the promise of wages for work—wages agreed upon in advance—make the individual possible for the first time in history: the individual *woman,* one might say.

MR. BELLOW'S CITY, AND OTHERS

> "In the end you can't save your soul and life by thought. But if you *think,* the least of the consolation prizes is the world."
>
> —EINHORN TO AUGIE
> *The Adventures of Augie March*

Yet the City does retain its aura of the sacred: it sometimes seems a place of godliness, if no longer a City of God. How else to account for the fascination of the literary mind with the City as a phenomenon—an outrage, a spectacle, an emblem of human ingenuity that seems frankly suprahuman? Quite apart from the somewhat mechanical fatalism of Stephan Crane, and the platitudinous pessimism of Dreiser; apart from the deeply moving novels of "social realism" of Anzia Yezierska and her contemporaries, and a more recent woman novelist of comparable power, Harriette Arnow,[12] one encounters a celebration of the City as an end in itself—an archetype of amoral dynamism that awakens no emotion more violently than that of simple awe.

William James's extravagant remarks on New York City are as valid for 1983 as for 1907:

> The first impression of New York . . . is one of repulsion at the clangor, disorder, and permanent earthquake conditions. But this time, installed . . . in the center of the cyclone, I caught the pulse

of the machine, took up the rhythm, and vibrated with, and found it simply magnificent. . . . The courage, the heaven-scaling audacity of it all, and the *lightness* withal, as if there was nothing that was not easy, and the great pulses and bounds of progress, so many in directions all simultaneous that the coordination is indefinitely future, give a kind of *drumming background* of life that I have never felt before. I'm sure that once *in* that movement, and at home, all other places would seem insipid. . . .[13]

One of the most remarkable achievements of James Joyce's *Ulysses*—more remarkable by far than the dazzling harlequinade of its styles and Homeric structure—is the rendering, in the most supple, sensuous, and precise language possible, of the city of Dublin: that city where "everyone knows everyone else." Joyce's great subject is less his people, memorable as they are, than his setting; that Dublin that is solely and specifically *that* Dublin, on June 16, 1904, with its dissonant harmony of Irish voices. Joyce's mystical nature would have it that God (even the hangman god) is "doubtless all in all in all of us," and that every life, in Stephen Dedalus's words, is "many days, day after day," but the glory of his novel is the city of Dublin itself. Joyce's boldly new art *renders* the city but refuses to *present* it: we experience Dublin in snatches and fragments, catching only glimpses of it, carried along by the momentum of Leopold's or Stephen's subjectivity: we know the city from the inside, though in a sense we "know" it hardly at all. The Dublin of *Ulysses* is subliminally granted. "Everything speaks in its own way," Bloom quietly observes. The City speaks through everyone and everything, in a multitude of voices.

"Moses Herzog" and "Charlie Citrine" are Joycean names, if not precisely Joycean people, but we should suspect in any case that Saul Bellow has learned from Joyce (as he has "learned" from any number of writers), for who among twentieth-century American novelists has evoked the City with more passion and more resonance than Bellow? With very little interest in formal experimentation, and no interest at all in following the wild, hilarious Dadaism of certain sections of *Ulysses* ("Nighttown" most famously), Bellow has nevertheless perfected a wonderfully supple and expressive style, a voice uniquely his own; one believes in Bellow immediately, no matter how fanciful the utterances of certain of his male characters. And they speak not simply for themselves but for their epochs, their cities. As the creator of superbly modulated prose and as the observer of character and cityscape Bellow is Joyce's equal. He has written no novel to rival *Ulysses*—who has?—but the complex riches of his numerous books attest to an imagination as deeply bound up with his subject as Joyce was with his; and if he is less ambitiously experimental than Joyce it should be noted that he is less self-indulgent as well. Augie March might be speaking for his creator in these arresting opening words of *The Adventures of Augie March:*

> I am an American, Chicago born—Chicago, that somber city— and go at things as I have taught myself, free-style, and will make the record in my own way: first to knock, first admitted; some- times an innocent knock, sometimes a not so innocent.

Augie March's Chicago—that of the slums and near-slums, of the 1920s and 30s—like Anzia Yezierska's Lower East Side, is a place of congestion and drama. European immigrants, blacks, even Mexi- cans, Jews, and Catholics, the Chicago of welfare clinics and ward politics—local millionaries—"bigshots and operators, commission- ers, grabbers, heelers, tipsters, hoodlums, wolves, fixers, plaintiffs, flatfeet, men in Western hats and women in lizard shoes and fur coats, hothouse and arctic drafts mixed up, brute things and airs of sex, evidence of heavy feeding and systematic shaving, of calcula- tions, grief, not-caring, and hopes of tremendous millions"[14]—all are eagerly observed by young Augie March, the near-orphan, the innocent who is also a thief, yet still innocent; the boy who senses himself "adoptable" by surrogate parents, yet battens on opposition. Augie is idealistic but he learns quickly the lessons of the City; to plot, to calculate, to negotiate, to press forward, never to allow himself to be manipulated, never to allow others to define his limits. As a young boy he is taught by his "Grandma" Lausch how to lie convincingly to administrators of a public health clinic; as a teenager he is initiated by his eccentric millionaire employer William Einhorn into the pleasure—the paid-for pleasure—of a downtown brothel. Given Augie's frequent romanticism we are surprised that his first sexual experience should pass by him so quickly, and that in summary ("when the thrill went off, like lightning smashed and dispersed into the ground, I knew it was basically only a transaction") but Augie's judgment is authoritative; he knows, being a city boy, that one must pay for everything; and that it doesn't matter. "Nor using what other people used. That's what city life is."[15]

Augie's comic-epic adventures, and his occasional adventures into the near-tragic, school him shrewdly in the strategies of city life. He is acquainted with people who read in German and French, are familiar with Nietzsche and Spengler; in another direction he is acquainted with criminals. "I touched all sides," Augie says, "and nobody knew where I belonged. I had no good idea about that myself." He is there to learn the "lessons and theories of power" in the great city of Chicago, confident (and with justification, as Bellow's career indicates) that these lessons and theories will be generally applicable. For every Augie March in the near-slums of Chicago there are hundreds of Studs Lonigans, but Augie—of course!—is the survivor, the prince, just as Bellow's unique synthesis of the humanistic and the tragic, his apparently effortless synthesis of the "classic" and the defiantly modern, greatly outdistances the time- and place-locked "naturalism" of James T. Farrell. Like his creator, Augie refuses to be "determined" beforehand. He defines himself; he declares himself a "Columbus of those near-at-hand," a defiantly laughing creature, uncorrupted even by his own diminution of faith. The "universal eligibility to be noble" informs most of his acts, and those of his ambitious brother Simon, no matter how frequently these acts cast the brothers down, and mock Grandma Lausch's inflated hopes for them. Chicago is America writ large, and the American legend is wonderfully seductive: why should one *not* succeed in becoming an American? "What did Danton lose his head for, or why was there a Napoleon," Augie asked passionately, "if it wasn't to make a nobility of us all?"

Darkened by a few degrees, Augie's adventures might well be tragic; his ebullience might swerve into mania, or angry despair. (In his youthful idealism he calls to mind the brilliant but doomed Von Humboldt Fleisher of *Humboldt's Gift*—and it is curious that Augie never declares himself a writer.) After all, Augie's mother is slow-witted, and she has been abandoned by her husband; one of Augie's brothers is an idiot who must be institutionalized; the March family is always on the brink of actual poverty. Yet Augie's freewheeling gregariousness manages to absorb (thanks to the elasticity of Bellow's prose) a number of troublesome things—the anti-Semitism of neighborhood Polish Catholics, the disappointments of numerous petty jobs and various sorties into amateur crime, and the gradual disintegration of the March family. For though Augie is very much a loner, *Augie March* is the most generously populated of novels. Chicago emerges as a city of giants who reveal themselves in their speech (eloquent, eccentric, lyric as any in *Ulysses)* and in their possessions (which, like Joyce, Bellow loves to catalog at length). They are reckless, tender, cunning, naïve, duplicitous, and loyal by turns. They may be, like the "great" Einhorn, assessed in classical terms, as Augie spiritedly aligns himself with the chroniclers of the great epics of the past: "I have the right," he says, "to praise Einhorn and not care about smiles of derogation from those who think the race no longer has in any important degree the traits we honor in [antiquity]." Or they may be, like Einhorn's son Dingbat, as gigantic in another direction, and as tenderly observed:

> Without being a hoodlum himself [Dingbat] was taken up with gang events and crime, a kind of amateur of the lore and done up in the gangster taste so that you might take him for somebody tied in with the dangerous Druccis or Big Hayes Hubacek: sharp financial hat, body-clasping suit, the shirt Andalusian style buttoned up to the collar and worn without a necktie, trick shoes, pointed and pimpy, polished like a tango dancer's; he clumped hard on the leather heels. Dingbat's hair was violent, brilliant, black, treated, ripple-marked. Bantam, thin-muscled, swift, almost frail, he had an absolutely unreasonable face. To be distinguished from brutal—it wasn't that, there was a kind of sentiment

in it. But wild, down-twisting, squint-eyed, unchangeable firm
and wrong in thoughts, with the prickles coming black through
his unmethodical after-shave talcum: the puss of an executioner's
subject. . . . [16]

Augie understands himself "forced early into deep city aims" in a
crowded environment that can, at any moment, turn against him.
"You do all you can to humanize and familiarize the world," Augie
observes, when his fortune declines, "and suddenly it becomes more
strange than ever." At the city college he attends for a while he finds
himself one of hundreds, or thousands, of the children of immigrants
from every part of Chicago, aspiring to be, "the idea was," *American*.
Which means to acquire power, by way of wealth, by way of the
manipulation of others. Augie resists this Americanization, but he
remains a child of Chicago, rather like the playwright Charlie Citrine
who cannot—for all his cosmopolitan fame—free himself of the
nostalgia for Chicago that is also a perverse fascination with and
celebration of mortality—death. Whether Bellow composed *Augie
March* for the sake of the many ideas it offers, or whether the ideas are
mere excuses for his masterful evocations of Chicago, the reader is
likely to be most struck by the young author's zestful attention to the
details of time and place. Who else would take time to celebrate the
"greatness of place" of Gary, Indiana; though Augie is temporarily
wretched he notes:

Docks and dumps of sulphur and coal, and flames seen by their
heat, not light, in the space of noon air among the black, huge
Pasiphaë cows and other columnar animals, headless, rolling a
rust of smoke and connected in an enormous statuary of hearths
and mills—here and there an old boiler or a hill of cinders in the
bulrush spawning-holes of frogs. . . . Thirty crowded miles on
oil-spotted road, where the furnace, gas, and machine volcanoes
cooked the Empedocles fundamentals into pig iron, girders, and
rails. . . .[17]

"If I mentioned a Chicago junkyard as well as Charlemagne's estate,"
says Augie defensively, "I had my reasons. For should I look into any
air, I could recall the bees and gnats of dust in the heavily divided heat

of a street of El pillars—such as Lake Street, where the junk and old bottle-yards are—like a terribly conceived church of madmen. . . . And sometimes misery came over me to feel that I myself was the creation of such places."[18]

In the long story "Looking for Mr. Green" in the volume *Mosby's Memoirs* (1951) the native-born Chicagoan George Grebe is employed by the Welfare Department to deliver checks in the Negro district—but he cannot find the crippled black man Green, no matter how courageously or how desperately he tries. The black slums of Chicago will not yield their secrets to him; he *cannot* find the possibly mythical Green. But in his search he learns of a world, and of people, that he had not previously encountered. (He is a university graduate, with a degree in Classics worthless in the Depression years; his father was a butler in the home of a Lake Shore millionaire.) On the walls of tenement buildings he reads enigmatic scrawls as if they contained a message for him: "So the sealed rooms of pyramids were decorated, and the caves of human dawn." Grebe is one of Bellow's characteristic heroes—ingenuous, eager to be instructed, eager to be of aid. He does not resent his supervisor's amused remarks on the ironies of "superior" education in this "fallen world of appearances": "I'll tell you, as a man of culture," Raynor says pompously, "that though nothing looks to be real, and everything stands for something else, and that thing for a still further thing—there ain't any comparison between $25 and $37 a week, regardless of the last reality." Nor did the Greeks, for all their thoughtfulness, care to part with their slaves.

Herzog is a richly textured and extremely intense novel about an urban man, Moses Herzog, who shuttles back and forth between Chicago and New York, negotiating the terms of a most unpleasant divorce as he comes closer and closer to a breakdown. Perhaps he is already out of his mind—which is all right with him. At the novel's end, after some feverish activity, Herzog retreats to his mortgaged country home in Ludeyville, Massachusetts, with "no messages for anyone."

Like Augie March, Herzog consciously resists the temptation to be heroic—to be involved in a dramatic (and consequently artificial) sequence of acts. The novel's theme is central to Bellow's mature work, and is stated quite explicitly midway in the narrative: "The real and essential question is one of our employment by other human beings and their employment by us. Without this true employment you never dread death, you cultivate it. . . ."[19] In the foreground, however, *Herzog* is near-constant motion. Herzog is always going up or down subway steps, hailing taxis, flying in airplanes, driving (with unfortunate consequences) the Chicago freeway. A highly articulate intellectual—a historian—Herzog manages to get himself arrested by the Chicago police for possession of an old revolver; he is very badly treated by his former wife Madeleine and her somewhat comic lover; but he retreats finally to the fairly plausible "idyllic" setting of Ludeyville and—so it would seem—saves himself from collapse.

Herzog is an unusually self-absorbed novel, far more of an extended monologue than Bellow's other works, and one catches hardly more than glimpses of Herzog's Chicago, though he admits to being deeply involved with it. *His* Chicago, as he says sentimentally, is the Woodlawn Avenue section of Hyde Park:

> Massive, clumsy, amorphous, smelling of mud and decay, dog turds; sooty facades, slabs of structural *nothing,* senselessly ornamented triple porches with huge cement urns for flowers that contained only rotting cigarette butts and other stained filth; sun parlors under tiled gables, rank areaways, gray backstairs, seamed and ruptured concrete from which sprang grass; ponderous four-by-four fences that sheltered growing weeds. [Here] Herzog did feel at home. He was perhaps as midwestern and unfocused as these same streets. (Not so much determinism, he thought, as a lack of determining elements—the absence of a formative power.)[20]

Driving to his elderly stepmother's home he broods over "clumsy, stinking, tender Chicago," and notes a species of flower he imagines to be peculiar to Chicago: "crude, waxy things like red and purple crayon bits, in a special class of false-looking natural objects." These foolish plants touch Herzog because they are so "graceless, so corny."

By contrast, there is nothing tender, nothing remotely redemptive, about the City of *Mr. Sammler's Planet*—which is to say, New York City. As one of the "great" cities of the civilized world it is sharply disappointing: its hold on civilization is extremely tenuous. Not only does society appear to be sinking into madness, but there is, as well, the *excuse* of madness. Sammler passes judgment on a "whole nation, all of civilized society . . . seeking the blameless state of madness. The privileged, almost aristocratic state of madness."[21] As if to mock Bellow's high intentions, an opportunistic young man tells Sammler: "You should denounce New York City. You should speak like a prophet, like from another world."

Mr. Sammler's Planet shares with *Humboldt's Gift*, and parts of *Herzog*, a curious and sometimes uneasy wedding of high, grave, and indeed "prophetic" musings and a plot that is frequently farcical, populated by comic characters. Elderly, half-blind, a distinguished historian and journalist, Artur Sammler looks back upon his friendship with another prophet, H. G. Wells, and his acquaintance with Bloomsbury; he looks back, with distinctly less pleasure, on the madness of Nazism, the concentration camps, and a death ditch in Poland in which he almost died. He is a seer, a voice: he exists primarily in his judgments, which are quite savage. Perhaps it is a consequence of his age, as well as the high degree of reflective intelligence he represents, that he is an observer throughout the novel—a protagonist whose passivity and ironic cast of mind alienate him from the City, and forbid him much sympathy with it. The self-absorbed energies of the great city have lost their power to fascinate in the 1960s: too much is happening, very little is comprehended or absorbed, there is a "sexual madness" in the air, and in Sammler's words, "You could see the suicidal impulses of civilization pushing strongly." Like anyone who has seen the world collapse once, Sammler entertains the possibility that it might collapse twice.

Though Sammler's reading consists solely of Meister Eckhardt and the Bible (anticipating, perhaps, Charlie Citrine's "mystical" learnings) he is very much aware of the chaos around him, and is in fact caught up with it, in the sometimes strained plot Bellow has devised to illuminate one facet of the decade's absurdity. Sammler feels like the time-traveler in Wells's fantasy *The Time Machine,* and though the curve of the novel brings him to a thematic (and heavily rhetorical) affirmation of this life, this earth—in short, this *planet*— the novel's vitality springs from his general repulsion. This is the symbolic City in which a rat can be mistaken for a dachshund, and sexual experimentation of various kinds is taken up on principle. Simply living in New York makes Sammler think compulsively of Sodom and Gomorrah—a general doom "desired by people who have botched everything." Can the individual transcend this social malaise? Is there a margin of human accountability, quite apart from the lawlessness of civilization's "leaders"? But how, bewitched by the frenzy of the age, is one to "meet the terms of his contract"?

Perhaps because it was written during a particularly tumultuous decade, in which the fairly conservative Saul Bellow was frequently attacked for his political beliefs, *Mr. Sammler's Planet* is the harshest of his novels. It is filled with brooding upon evil and the fascination of evil; the author makes no attempt to link his protagonist with the City, except as an accidental witness; we have come a great distance from the exuberance of young Augie March. Even Sammler's musings upon slum life (as seen from his nephew Elya's Rolls-Royce) are oddly devoid of a sense of human kinship with the "underprivileged":

Downtown on Broadway . . . Tenements, the Puerto Rican squalor. Then the University, squalid in a different way. . . . Except on special occasions . . . Sammler never came this way any more. Walking for exercise, he didn't venture this far uptown. And now . . . he inspected the subculture of the underprivileged (terminology recently acquired in the *New York Times),* its Caribbean fruits, its plucked naked chickens with loose necks and eyelids blue, the wavering fumes of Diesel and hot lard. Then Ninety-sixth Street, tilted at all four corners, the kiosks and movie houses, the ramparts of wire-fastened newspaper bundles, and the colors of panic waving. Broadway . . . always challenged Sammler. He was never up to it. And why should there be any contest? But there was, every time. For something was stated here. By a

convergence of all minds and all movements the conviction
transmitted by this crowd seemed to be that reality was a terrible
thing, and that the final truth about mankind is overwhelming
and crushing. This vulgar, cowardly conclusion, rejected by
Sammler with all his heart, was the implicit local orthodoxy, the
populace itself being metaphysical and living out this interpretation of reality and this view of truth. . . . Broadway at Ninety-
sixth Street gave him such a sense of things. Life, when it was like
this, all question-and-answer from the top of intellect to the very
bottom, was really a state of singular dirty misery. . . . This
poverty of soul, its abstract state, you could see in the faces on the
street. And he too had a touch of the same disease. . . .[22]

A Schopenhauerian vision. But even here, in this frenzied running-
down corner of civilization, one can, by the very act of *thinking*,
detach oneself from the fury of the world's blind Will: by way of the
Idea which is not overpowered by *maya* in any of its forms. The irony
of Sammler's (and Bellow's) position, freely acknowledged in the
looser, wilder *Humboldt's Gift*, is that the novel's energies depend
entirely upon the repulsiveness of what is being denounced. Nor is
the "fallen" world dramatized: it is *only* denounced.

Humboldt's Gift, which was published in 1975 and brought
Bellow, after a distinguished career, both the long-withheld Pulitzer
Prize and the Nobel Prize, resolves in comedy of a frequently
outsized, loony nature many of the tragic paradoxes of Sammler's
world. In *Humboldt's Gift*, discursive and moralizing passages seem,
at times, set down almost at random in the text, and the novel's
protagonist—Charlie Citrine, a "famous" and commercially successful playwright—often earns the impatience his ex-wives and other
critics ("Reality Instructors") feel for him. Yet beneath the carnival-
like plot there is the constant brooding upon death—mortality and
love and fame and death in America—that Bellow has elsewhere
explored; as Augie said long ago, "There is a darkness. It is for
everyone."

Humboldt is, of course, Von Humboldt Fleisher, the beautiful,
brilliant boy-genius of a poet who becomes—all too quickly, and too
plausibly—a disheveled ruin of an alcoholic whose fate is a lonely

death in a hotel off Times Square. Charlie Citrine, his old friend, is obsessed with Humboldt, not simply because he feels that, in complex ways, both he and Humboldt betrayed each other (and loved each other, like brothers), but because Humboldt's fate is illustrative of the fate of the poet in America at the present time:

> The country is proud of its dead poets [Citrine thinks]. It takes terrific satisfaction in the poets' testimony that the USA is too tough, too big, too much, too rugged, that American reality is overpowering. And to be a poet is a school thing, a skirt thing, a church thing. The weakness of the spiritual powers is proved in the childishness, madness, drunkenness, and despair of these martyrs. . . . Poets are loved, but loved because they just can't make it here. They exist to light up the enormity of the awful tangle and justify the cynicism of those who say, "If *I* were not such a corrupt, unfeeling bastard, creep, thief, and vulture, I couldn't get through this either. . . ." So this . . . is how successful bitter hard-faced and cannibalistic people exult.[23]

And Citrine is convinced that Chicago with its "gigantesque outer life" contains the problem of poetry and the inner life in America. For if power, fame, and money—but particularly power—are all that matter, how is the poet to compete as a man among men? (For Bellow's point has very much to do with competition.) Where once the poet was considered to have divine powers, now his relative impotence is shown for what it is: "Having no machines, no transforming knowledge comparable to the knowledge of Boeing or Sperry Rand or IBM or RCA. . . . For could a poem pick you up in Chicago and land you in New York two hours later? Or could it compute a space shot? It had no such powers. And interest was where power was. . . . It was not Humboldt, it was the USA that was making its point: 'Fellow Americans, listen. If you abandon materialism and the normal pursuits of life you wind up at Bellevue like this poor kook.' "[24]

Beneath Citrine's comic despair is the heart cry of Bellow himself, who has written elsewhere, frankly and thoughtfully, of the failure of the nation's "leaders" to pay the most minimal attention to novelists and humanists like himself. One hardly wants the State to show an interest in literature like that of Stalin's, yet the situation is rather discouraging for a writer of Bellow's stature. In a self-interview published in 1975, shortly after the appearance of *Humboldt's Gift,* Bellow attacks the "formulae, the jargon, the exciting fictions, the heightened and dramatized shadow events" selected by the media and accepted by the public and "believed by almost everyone to be real." Is the reading of serious literature at all possible for such people? In the universities, where one might expect something very different, "the teaching of literature has been a disaster." Interpretation—critical methodology—"learned" analyses—are substituted for the actual experience of the work of art itself. And the cultural intelligentsia (professors, commentators, editors) have become politicized and analytical in temper, and hostile to literature: the members of this elite, Bellow says, *had* literature in their student days and are now well beyond it.[25]

The City of *Humboldt's Gift* is background primarily, experienced in snatched moments, though greatly bound up with Citrine's meditation upon death. (Indeed, *Humboldt's Gift* is a novel whose very spirit feeds upon a sustained communion with the dead.) Citrine is not so obsessed with his guilt over Humboldt and his love for Renata, however, that he fails to pause for characteristically Bellovian moments of sharply observed commentary: New York City, for instance, seen from a high window of the Plaza Hotel, reveals itself in its myriad dazzling lights as similar to "cells in a capillary observed through a microscope, elastically changing shape, bumping and pulsatory"; and, in one of the book's strongest passages, Citrine broods:

> On hot nights Chicagoans feel the city body and soul. The stockyards are gone, Chicago is no longer slaughter-city, but the old smells revive in the night heat. Miles of railroad siding along the streets once were filled with red cattle cars, the animals waiting to enter the yards lowing and reeking. The old stink still haunts the place. It returns at times, suspiring from the vacated soil, to remind us all that Chicago had once led the world in butcher-

technology and that billions of animals had died here. And that night the windows were open wide and the familiar depressing multilayered stink of meat, tallow, blood-meal, pulverized bones, hides, soap, smoked slabs, and burnt hair came back. Old Chicago breathed again. . . . I heard fire trucks and . . . ambulances, bowel-deep and hysterical. In the surrounding black slums incendiarism shoots up in summer. . . . Chicago, this night, was panting, the big urban engines going, tenements blazing in Oakwood with great shawls of flame, the sirens weirdly yelping, the fire engines, ambulances, and police cars—mad-dog, gashing-knife weather, a rape and murder night. . . . Bands of kids prowled with hand-guns and knives. . . . [26]

Have we come full circle, to the demonic subhuman City of Stephen Crane's *Maggie*?

Yet Citrine, and presumably Bellow, would leave us with the conviction that the individual is, indeed, capable of transcending the physical limits set for him by the City. Citrine appears convinced—as a consequence of his reading in the mystic Rudolf Steiner, and his involvement with people out of his and Humboldt's shared past—that one's existence is "merely the present existence, one in a series," and that there is more to any experience, connection, or relationship than ordinary consciousness, the daily life of the ego, can grasp. "The soul belongs," Citrine says, "to a greater, an all-embracing life outside. . . ."

The City has so fascinated contemporary writers of prose and poetry alike that no single essay can do justice to the variety of "images" that has been explored. Some are deservedly famous, like Bellow's, and that of Ralph Ellison (whose *Invisible Man* of 1952 is still very much a contemporary work); others, for instance Anne Tyler's Baltimore, deserve closer attention. Philip Levine has written less of Detroit than of lives passed in the haze of Detroit's industrial slums and near-slums; his most powerful poems fairly pulse with the beat of that infinitely sprawling city, and take their life from a perverse nostalgia which is all the more disturbing for its authenticity:

Coming Home, Detroit, 1968

A winter Tuesday, the city pouring fire,
Ford Rouge sulfurs the sun, Cadillac, Lincoln,
Chevy gray. The fat stacks
of breweries hold their tongues. Rags,
papers, hands, the stems of birches
dirited with words.

                                    Near the freeway
you stop and wonder what came off,
recall the snowstorm where you lost it all,
the wolverine, the northern bear, the wolf
caught out, ice and steel raining
from the foundries in a shower
of human breath. On sleds in the false sun
the new material rests. One brown child
stares and stares into your frozen eyes
until the lights change and you go
forward to work. The charred faces, the eyes
boarded up, the rubble of innards, the cry
of wet smoke hanging in your throat,
the twisted river stopped at the color of iron.
We burn this city every day.[27]

New York City—that most mythical of cities—tends to emerge
in recent literature as hellish, or at any rate murderous; yet its
presence is the occasion for some of the most subtle and intelligently
graceful prose of our time. Consider Hortense Calisher's classic "The
Scream on 57th Street" in which a lonely woman hears, or believes
she hears, a scream of terror five flights below her bedroom window:
Some of us, Mrs. Hazlitt thinks with desperate pride, *are still responsi-
ble.*[28] Consider the New York observed in Renata Adler's novel of
anecdote and collage, *Speedboat* (in which an unsolved murder is
noted—but is not dwelt upon); and the New York of Elizabeth
Hardwick's *Sleepless Nights* (in which another murder—among numerous disturbing events—is noted in passing). The city cannot be
comprehended but the vertiginous nature of its threat can be
translated into language—a language necessarily oblique, circum-

spect, even coy. In Donald Barthelme's prose poems the City is reimagined from every possible angle: its suprahuman dynamism is a given, like the Milky Way, like the passage of time. A typically anonymous Barthelme hero sets out upon a "legendary" quest one day, hoping to climb the glass mountain (which might be confused with a high-rise office building) on the corner of Thirteenth Street and Eighth Avenue. At the base of the mountain are the corpses of innumerable knights who have died attempting this climb, but the hero perseveres, and at the top—after ninety-odd numbered sentences—he encounters the "beautiful enchanted symbol" in its golden castle. He approaches the symbol with its "layers of meaning" but, unfortunately, when he touches it "it changed into only a beautiful princess" whom he then throws headfirst down the mountain and into the street.[29]

In another Barthelme fantasy, "The Balloon," a gigantic balloon appears in Manhattan, covering forty-five blocks north–south and an irregular area east–west, about six crosstown blocks on either side of Fifth Avenue. The Balloon is an anticity, an artifice of the imagination, hence disturbingly controversial. Everyone contemplates it; everyone has a theory. But it is reasonable to assume that the balloon's fascination lies partly in the fact that it is not limited or defined. It changes constantly. "The ability of the balloon to shift its shape, to change, was very pleasing, especially to people whose lives were rather rigidly patterned, persons to whom change, although desired, was not available. The balloon, for the twenty-two days of its existence, offered the possibility, in its randomness, of mislocation of the self, in contradistinction to the grid of precise, rectangular pathways under our feet."[30]

In "City Life" the anonymous narrator expresses a view of the City not dissimilar to Arthur Sammler's: it is muck, but a multidirectional muck with its own mayor. It is a creation of the muckish nation-state, in itself the creation of that muck of mucks, human consciousness. And in one of Barthelme's most elaborately pessimistic stories, "Brain Damage," a finale of despair takes on the rhythms of a litany: "There's brain damage on the horizon, a great big blubbery cloud of it coming this way—This is the country of brain damage . . . these are the rivers of brain damage . . . where the damaged pilots land the big, damaged ships. . . . Skiing along on the soft surface of brain damage, never to sink, because we don't understand the danger—"[31]

In one of the penultimate stories of the elegiac *Too Far to Go*, John Updike positions his soon-to-be-divorced protagonist Richard Maple in a Boston apartment with a view of a locally famous skyscraper. This skyscraper is a beautiful disaster, never completed, and Richard, in his solitude, finds much to contemplate in it. The skyscraper is disastrous—glass keeps falling from it—precisely because it is beautiful. "The architect had had a vision. He had dreamed of an invisible building, though immense; the glass was meant to reflect the sky and the old low brick skyline of Boston, and to melt into the city. Instead, the windows of mirroring glass kept falling to the street, and were replaced by ugly opacities of black plywood." Richard comes to equate the skyscraper with his own soul: even unseen, it is always present.

One day, however, Richard takes a walk, and finds himself at the base of the skyscraper. A mistake: the skyscraper close up is hideous.

> Heavily planked and chicken-wired tunnels, guarded by barking policemen, protected pedestrians from falling glass. . . . Trestles and trucks jammed the cacophonous area. The lower floors were solid plywood, of a Stygian black; the building, so lovely in air, had tangled mucky roots.[32]

The building, so lovely in air, had tangled mucky roots.

"At Least I Have Made a Woman of Her"

IMAGES OF WOMEN IN
YEATS, LAWRENCE, FAULKNER

O may she live like some green laurel
Rooted in one dear perpetual place.

—W. B. YEATS
"A Prayer for My Daughter"

A man's quarrel with Woman is his quarrel with himself—with those "despised" and muted elements in his personality which he cannot freely acknowledge because they challenge his sense of masculine supremacy and control. Modernist literature, despite its extraordinary sophistication in technical literary terms—its openness to radical re-visionings of the act of "storytelling," its delight in linguistic and structural experimentation—exhibits nonetheless most of the received and unexamined values of popular mass culture, so far as images of Woman are concerned; it is not an exaggeration to argue that Modernist fiction carries over deep-rooted nineteenth-century prejudices of a distinctly bourgeois sort. Morality is examined in the light of new and radical interpretations of what the world "is," but these interpretations are as fixed in masculinity as ever. From Yeats's sacred ideal of femininity (famously expressed in "A Prayer for My Daughter") to Lawrence's phallic mysticism; from the misogynous bias of Eliot and Conrad to Faulkner's crude portraits of mammalian beauties or castrating "neuters" who deserve death, the most celebrated of twentieth-century writers have presented Woman through the distorting lens of sexist imagination—sometimes with courtly subtlety, sometimes with a ferocious indignation that erupts in violence. The paradox with which the feminist critic or sympathizer must contend is this: that revolutionary advances in literature often fail to transcend deeply conservative and stereotypical images of women, as if, in a sense, the nineteenth century were eerily superimposed upon even the most defiantly inventive literary "visions" of the twentieth century.

"MODERNISM" AND (DESPISED) "POPULAR CULTURE"

By Modernism we mean a heterogeneous and not easily characterized movement in literature that involved extraordinary innovations in style, ebullient new uses of language, and a radical redefining of what is meant by "Art"; what is meant by the "individual," the "artist," "society," and "reality" itself. We think immediately of the bold Symbolist affirmation of the soul in its dreaming and frequently hallucinatory states: the private Soul, that is, in contrast to the public Self. We think of Oscar Wilde's declaration that Art is not only superior to Life and to Nature, but unrelated to both. Art is "the telling of beautiful untrue things" and is synonymous with lying: it is expected to exhibit not sincerity but skill. At the core of the Modernist sensibility is the ecstatic monomaniacal devotion of Flaubert to his craft—Flaubert, who loved the difficult and addictive act of writing to the degree to which, it seems, he loathed life. "We must love one another in Art, as the mystics love one another in God": a statement of such appeal for any writer that I am always willing to extirpate it from its pragmatic context.[1]

Modernism is justly seen as revolutionary in its insistence upon the subjective, the unique, the elevation of the Artist as the priest of a new dispensation, and its militant hero as well. The Artist-Hero is one who, in Yeats's persuasive words, descends into the terrifying and uncharted depths of the soul as other heroes have, by tradition, entered physical combat. Yeats argues: "Because an emotion does not exist, or does not become perceptible and active among us, till it has found its expression, in color or in form or in sound . . . and because these modulations . . . evoke the same emotion, poets and painters and writers . . . are continually making and un-making mankind"[2]—a remarkable statement, no less iconoclastic for its being so moderately phrased. (And who is to say, if we add to Yeats's brief list *the purveyors of popular culture in a democratic society,* that he isn't correct?) The Artist-Priest of James Joyce's aesthetic is the more reasonably empowered with "sacred" faculties, in that the object of his life's vocation is not a fantastical spirit-world of wistful and childlike yearnings (that is, traditional religion as handed down by a priesthood or blessed clergy), but *this* world—the very world in which we live physically and emotionally, rendered in all its detail, with no more revulsion for the contradictory, the obscene, the vulgar, the unspeakable, than any anthropologist or chemist might feel confronted with his or her primary material.

This is a revolutionary attitude that strikes us in the waning decades of the twentieth century as so inevitable, so obvious, that it scarcely needs to be reiterated, like many of the defiant pronouncements of Modernism. (To which we might add the pronouncements of the Symbolists, the Surrealists, and even the Dadaists, whose battles have all been—perhaps Pyrrhically—won.) The fundamental supposition is that the Artist's mind does not passively *experience* the world; it energetically *constructs* (or *reconstructs*) it. Vision translates into style; personality translates into voice; all art is or should be experimental if it is to be judged worthy of our attention. (As Joyce's Stephen Dedalus somewhat dogmatically states, the evolution of a highly self-conscious art brings with it a paradoxical transcendence of the personal or autobiographical, yet, as it is imbued with the distinctive voice of genius, it becomes the highest possible expression of personality—if style and personality are identical.)

The prejudices of the bourgeois culture are to be overthrown, rejected, ignored, transcended: for the tiresome pieties of the Victorians, like those of the Augustans, having to do with the morality of art, and the duties of the artist, and the servile role of literature in society, are judged as not simply contemptible but mistaken. " . . . I might be expected to speak of the social, that is to say sociological or political, obligation of the poet," says Wallace Stevens. "He has none."

In its aesthetics as well as in its actual products Modernism constituted something radically new in literary history.

By contrast, what we know as "popular" or "mass" culture has always conformed to the most insipid prejudices, and the least subtle formulations, of society. Its wares are soiled with frequent handling; its styles are so hackneyed, trite, and homogeneous, they constitute a single style; it is as incapable of artistic experimentation as of moral and intellectual experimentation. "The greatest appeal to the greatest number" is the standard, and no idiosyncratic vision is recommended. Mass culture, particularly in our time, is not so much *created* as *produced,* like tissue paper or soft drinks; and this ephemeral quality is actually desirable since, in a consumer-oriented society, the healthy market is one in which products are not viable for very long. One buys, one uses, one discards, one again buys: a ceaseless present tense, an ideal amnesia.

Where Modernism held the uniqueness of the work of art to be sacrosanct, and a life's devotion to the perfection of craft a life well spent, popular culture is an expression of the faith in *interchangeable parts* and *ceaseless production*—for the assembly line should never be shut down. The "vision" of the redoubtable American prophet Henry Ford might well be translated into a cogent if abbreviated philosophical system, its central thesis having to do with perpetual motion (factories never shut down, conveyor belts never halted, raw materials never exhausted, power never depleted, consumers never *fully* satisfied—for the ideal is a civilization of self-consuming "products," a whirligig of sheer energy).

As instructive as these warring visions of the Unique and the Interchangeable are the contrasting attitudes toward money. Modernism turns its back on commercial success, taking pride in the small and sometimes near-nonexistent audiences its most difficult products have drawn; Popular Culture is really concerned with nothing else. Money may be a kind of poetry, as Wallace Stevens enigmatically said, but is poetry a kind of money?—surely not. Indeed, if one becomes even modestly popular this is a symptom, in the eyes of Modernist and Postmodernist sensibilities, of the necessarily inferior nature of one's art. Though liberal and even radical politically, the Modernist temperament is defiantly elitist otherwise, for it is a truism that the "mass mind" is incapable of valuing or even recognizing excellence; hence it follows that whatever pleases the greatest numbers must be despicable. And surely there is a plethora of painful examples to buttress this argument. For instance, Melville enjoyed early commercial success with his fast-paced and guileless "adventure" tales, the exotic *Typee* and *Omoo,* and, as his art increased in ambition, complexity, and darkness of vision (in *Moby Dick, Pierre, The Confidence-Man,* among others), he drifted into absolute obscurity—he simply ceased to exist as a force in American letters. Henry James had to endure the humiliation of declining sales throughout his long and industrious career, and though it is hardly surprising that *The Ambassadors, The Wings of the Dove,* and *The Golden Bowl* should sell painfully less than *Daisy Miller,* it is scarcely encouraging to fellow writers.

Opposed as Modernism and Popular Culture are in these and many other respects, it is always something of a shock to see in which ways their tacit prejudices overlap. The fundamental assumption, for instance, of what being *female* involves—and how social roles are so imbued with a mystique of biological determinism that they are not perceived as "roles" at all.

"Women are to be protected, respected, supported, and petted"—this is the jocular advice given, presumably to gentlemen, in *The American Book of Manners* (1880), one of countless best-selling books of its kind published in the post-Civil War years. Hundreds of thousands of such manuals were sold in the United States in the second half of the nineteenth century, as the division between social classes—between the well-to-do and the great army of the poor—

became more pronounced. Genteel anxiety evidently focused upon the problem of what constitutes a *lady*. The Christian duties and obligations of wife and mother; how to comport oneself in society; how to be a helpmeet (if female) to one's spouse; even how to be patriotic in the most feminine, which is to say the least effective, way—

> In our own sphere, the hearth beside,
>   The patriot's heart to cheer;—
> The young, unfolding mind to guide,—
>   The future sage to rear;
> Where sleeps the cradled infant fair,
> To watch with love, and kneel in prayer—
> Bless each sad soul with pity's smile,
> And frown on every latent wile
> That threats the pure, domestic shade,
> Sister—so best our life shall aid
> The land we love.[3]

Women assiduously studied such popular books as *The Young Woman's Guide, The Young Mother,* and *The Young Wife,* all by a gentleman by the name of Dr. William Alcott; *The American Lady* by Charles Butler was also consulted, dealing, as it did, with "the importance of the female character" and "considerations antecedent to marriage." *The Lady's Vase, Letters to Young Ladies, The Gentle Art of Pleasing, The Christian Home, The Young Lady's Friend, The Young Lady's Companion, The Lady's Guide to Perfect Gentility* . . . Marriage was endlessly discussed, but always in terms of duties and responsibilities: Woman's natural role was one of unquestioning subservience, docility, and sacrifice. One of the most famous of "marriage manuals" was Dr. George N. Naphey's *The Physical Life of Woman: Advice to the Maiden, Wife, and Mother* (1869, at the time of its first edition), a document that says very little about the physical life as we know it but is rich in vaporous pseudoreligious rhetoric. When a popular English periodical called *Chamber's Journal* ran a series of articles on the subject "A Woman's Thoughts About Women" in 1857, the (anonymous) thoughts were of this sort:

Dependence is in itself an easy and pleasant thing: dependence upon one we love perhaps the very sweetest thing in the world. To resign oneself totally and contentedly into the hand of another; to have no longer any need of asserting one's rights or one's personality, knowing that both are as precious to that other as they were to ourselves; to cease taking thought about oneself at all, and rest safe, at ease, assured that in great things and small we shall be guided and cherished, guarded and helped—in fact thoroughly "taken care of"—how delicious this all is. . . .[4]

The generally unquestioned attitude toward women was succinctly expressed by Robert Bell in *The Ladder of Gold* (1850): "Stern and obdurate strength is not the finest characteristic of women; they are most strong and most lovable in their weakness. . . . Even their errors and failures add a grace to our devotion by leaving something for our magnanimity to forgive."[5]

Another observer asserts that while "a thinking man is his own legislator and confessor, and obtains his own absolution, the woman, let alone the girl, does not have the measure of ethics in herself. She can only act if she keeps within the limits of morality, following what society has established as fitting"—a judgment we should dismiss as smug bigotry, did we not know that it was made by Freud.[6] If "superior" women were granted existence—superior in terms of their virtue, that is—they were likely to be figures from comfortably distant epochs, like the Middle Ages, that mythological bastion of faith and absolute stability.[7]

The cherished double standard, by which women are measured against ethereal expectations, and men granted their "manliness," never seems to be acknowledged in popular nonfiction or fiction of the nineteenth centry: the contemporary critic searches in vain, and resorts in the end to the expedient of calling much of the work duplicitous.[8] Romances and melodramas written with a female audience in mind, nearly always by female writers, selling in the hundreds of thousands of copies in the second half of the nineteenth century, presented a veritable army of stereotypical heroines, heroes, and villains, in various combinations and permutations of plot, not unlike those of standard soap opera. Of all writers no one, not even pornographers, is held more in contempt than the female novelists of the "popular-sentimental" school, that gaggle of "scribbling women" condemned by Hawthorne, who naïvely imagined that he was losing his audience to them. (In fact Hawthorne, along with Thoreau, Emerson, and Melville, had never one-tenth of this enormous middle-class audience.) Duplicitous, hypocritical, or utterly sincere in their service of resigning women to a patriarchal fate?—one can't be altogether certain in examining these writers, who in any case soon begin to blur into one another. There are Mrs. E. D. E. N. Southworth, who wrote more than sixty novels; Mary Jane Holmes, of whose forty novels two million copies were sold; Mrs. Augusta Jane Evans, whose best seller was *St. Elmo* (1866); Mrs. Elizabeth Stuart Phelps Ward, the prodigiously successful author of *The Gates Ajar* (1868); and many another, usually equipped with three or four names and the imprimatur "Mrs."

The world of the popular-sentimental novel is not so alien as contemporary feminist readers might wish to think. If there are passages of genuine literary merit in the interstices of the ludicrous steamroller plots, buried here and there amid interminable moraliz- ing speeches, they are likely to be descriptive: sudden, illuminating, and altogether fascinating pictures of domestic female life, private life, sequestered from male eyes. (Mrs. Southworth is particularly valuable in allowing us to overhear the exchanges between women and their servants, in some cases their slaves.) In general, however, even the most patient reader is likely to be numbed by the relentless moral tone, the sermonizing on Christian virtues of wifely submis- sion in the face of infidelity, drunkenness, and occasional violence. (Are men violent? If so, it is their nature. Should they be forgiven? Of course. One marries "for better and for worse, in sickness and in health." These are serious vows. Permanent vows. At least so far as the woman is concerned.)

Certainly these are cautionary tales, exempla, striking more closely to the bone (my metaphor is deliberate) than the chill, fastidiously controlled, the ultimately *merely* allegorical fictions by

Hawthorne. Or is *The Scarlet Letter,* with its patina of guilt, remorse, and redemption, yet another cautionary tale, couched in discreetly "unreal" language? And is the fate of the luxuriantly beautiful Zenobia of *The Blithedale Romance* meant to be instructive? Woman's *place* is in man's *world.*

In a representative novel by Mrs. Southworth, *The Discarded Daughter; or, The Children of the Isle,* a woman who is physically abused by her tyrannical husband disguises her injuries and passes them off as her own fault. ("No, Milly; no, my arm is not hurt, Milly," the long-suffering Mrs. Garnet declares, "I—I *fell,* Milly, and struck my head, I *think.* General Garnet had the presence of mind to bleed me—and perhaps that saved my life.") The brute returns to "bleed" her a second time, but Mrs. Garnet's Christian love is such that she not only forgives him for his cruelty but assures him that it isn't cruelty, the injury is her own fault, what seems to have occurred between them never occurred at all. The husband's reply: "It is dangerous, Alice, dangerous, to rebel either by stratagem or force against just authority."[9] Mrs. Southworth's heroine is clearly meant to be a model for her female readers not only in her acquiescence to her husband's brutality but in her steadfast denial—even to concerned friends—that anything is wrong. Naturally at her death she will be proclaimed a saint.

Yet the popular-sentimental novels do tend to blur, to grow hazy, to acquire in the memory a single style, not the voices of individual women so much as the overwrought hectoring of the victim giving "advice" and consolation to fellow victims. One cannot really fault the contempt of the "serious" male writer for these vaporous female concoctions, in which potentially tragic conflict is routinely resolved by embarrassing plot-turns: rightful heirs appear on schedule; the illegitimate child is revealed as—legitimate after all; a villain dies, hoisted on his own petard; a long-lost love miraculously returns; the glorious wedding takes place amid suitable festivity. The only admirable *female* is a *lady,* though tomboys of a sort are treated fondly, so long as they remain children. Bodies scarcely exist but clothes are everywhere in evidence, indefatigably

described. Here is a world of shameless insipid romance in which
platitudes are uttered on every page. ("Love can redeem any soul; it
was LOVE that gave itself for *all* souls! Love is religion—for 'God is
Love.' "[10]) Here is a world of female delusion in which individuality
is dissolved into types, and the eye's reading of the face is never to be
corrected. Consider Elsie in the "bloom of her young womanhood"—

> In form, she was rather above the medium height, of small frame,
> delicate, but not thin, for the round and small bones were well
> covered with soft, elastic flesh, that rounded and tapered off in the
> true line of beauty to the slender wrists and ankles. Her neck and
> bosom were beautiful beyond all poetic dreams of beauty, sug-
> gesting sweet thoughts of love, truth, and repose. Her hair was
> rich and abundant, falling in a mass of warm-hued, golden,
> auburn ringlets. Her eyes were dark blue, large and languishing.
> Her complexion was very fair, but warming in the cheek and lips
> into a faint but beautiful flush; the prevailing tone of her counte-
> nance was half-devotional, half-voluptuous; indeed, the nature of
> every ardent temperament is luxurious or saintly, as moral and
> mental tone gives it a bias; in hers, both were blended and the
> general character of her whole face and form, air and manner,
> was—HARMONY. There was no warring, no discord, not one
> dissonant element in that pure, that spiritualized, yet proud
> nature. She seemed . . . even when talking and hearing others talk,
> to be only half-given to the world; to be wrapped in the vision of
> some delicious, some blissful secret; to possess some hidden
> spring of joy; to have some secret, divine truth shrined in the
> temple of her heart, that elevated her expression to an exalted
> spirituality.[11]

Elsie also possesses a "tiny, snow-white hand" and an arm that is
"pure and fresh."

Yet another ideal feminine type—

> It must not be supposed that Mrs. Gould's mind was masculine. A
> woman with a masculine mind is not a being of superior effi-
> ciency; she is simply a phenomenon of imperfect differentiation—
> interestingly barren and without importance. [Mrs. Gould's]

intelligence being feminine led her to achieve the conquest of
Sulaco, simply by lighting the way for her unselfishness and
sympathy. She could converse charmingly but was not talkative.
The wisdom of the heart having no concern with the erection or
demolition of theories any more than with the defence of prejudices, has no random words at its command. The words it
pronounces have the value of acts of integrity, tolerance, and
compassion. A woman's true tenderness, like the true virility of
man, is expressed in action of a conquering kind.[12]

Interesting to note, too, that in this passage, Conrad's language is not
discernibly superior to that of the despised Mrs. Southworth. And
there are many such passages in Conrad.

One of the most highly regarded of Modernist poems is Yeats's
"A Prayer for My Daughter," written in 1919. If we examine it
closely we see that it carries both a blessing and a curse, though it is
the blessing critics always recall:

> I have walked and prayed for this young child an hour
> And heard the sea-wind scream upon the tower,
> And under the arches of the bridge, and scream
> In the elms above the flooded stream;
> Imagining in excited reverie
> That the future years had come,
> Dancing to a frenzied drum,
> Out of the murderous innocence of the sea.
>
> May she be granted beauty and yet not
> Beauty to make a stranger's eye distraught,
> Or hers before a looking-glass, for such,
> Being made beautiful overmuch,
> Consider beauty a sufficient end,
> Lose natural kindness and maybe
> The heart-revealing intimacy
> That chooses right, and never find a friend.

It is rarely remarked that Yeats's first concern for his daughter is her
physical appearance. He prays that she will be beautiful—but not *too*

beautiful—for such beauty might arouse in her a sense of her own autonomy: her existence in a "looking-glass" rather than in a man's eyes. Yeats goes on to hope, like many another anxious father, that his daughter will be spared passion and sensuality, for "It's certain that fine women eat/A crazy salad with their meat/Whereby the Horn of Plenty is undone." (The Horn of Plenty being, one must assume, an unintentional pun.)

Yeats had been in love, as all the world knows, with the beautiful and passionate Maud Gonne for many years; and had been so aroused by her revolutionary political views that, for a time, he had belonged to a secret extremist revolutionary group called the Irish Republican Brotherhood—in a remarkable defiance, in fact, of his own deeply introspective nature. Yet his prayer for his daughter is that she be chiefly learned in *courtesy*. And:

> May she become a flourishing hidden tree
> That all her thoughts may like the linnet be,
> And have no business but dispensing round
> Their magnanimities of sound,
> Nor but in merriment begin a chase,
> Nor but in merriment a quarrel.
> O may she live like some green laurel
> Rooted in one dear perpetual place.

This celebrated poet would have his daughter an object in nature for others'—which is to say male—delectation. She is not even an animal or a bird in his imagination but a vegetable: immobile, unthinking, placid, "hidden." The activity of her brain is analogous to the linnet's song—no distracting evidence of mental powers, only a "magnanimity" of sound, a kind of background music. The linnet with its modest brown plumage is surely not an accidental choice; a nightingale might have been summoned, too—except that the nightingale has been used too frequently in English poetry and is, in any case, a nocturnal creature. The poet's lifework is the creation of a distinct voice in which sound and sense are harmoniously wedded: the poet's daughter is to be brainless and voiceless, *rooted*.

So crushingly conventional is Yeats's imagination—and he is writing several decades after the despised Victorian women novelists—that he cannot conclude his prayer with this wish for his infant daughter; he must look into the future and anticipate her marriage. Though the ideal woman is childlike, in fact vegetative, with no passion, sensuality, or intelligence, it is the case that she must be given in marriage to a man: she will be incomplete unless she is joined "in custom and ceremony" to a husband.

> And may her bridegroom bring her to a house
> Where all's accustomed, ceremonious;
> For arrogance and hatred are the wares
> Peddled in the thoroughfares.
> How but in custom and in ceremony
> Are innocence and beauty born?
> Ceremony's a name for the rich horn,
> And custom for the spreading laurel tree.

This is the sentiment, not undercut but confirmed by the pat rhyming, of many a sentimental, "inspirational" poem of the nineteenth century. And the ideals of innocence and beauty, docility, spiritual muteness—altogether familiar to any student of popular literature.

This famous poem is not, however, solely a father's prayer, a gesture of sanctification: it is also a curse: an instrument of revenge. Though Yeats had written numberless poems celebrating Maud Gonne, primarily for her beauty ("Pallas Athene in that straight back and arrogant head"), he now says, in a stanza that strikes the ear as arbitrary:

> As intellectual hatred is the worst,
> So let her think opinions are accursed.
> Have I not seen the loveliest woman born
> Out of the mouth of Plenty's horn,
> Because of her opinionated mind
> Barter that horn and every good
> By quiet natures understood
> For an old bellows full of angry wind?

(One notes again the horn, and now the betrayal of the horn—the independent woman's most unspeakable act. But Yeats's imagery is for once not at his conscious command.)

The feminine soul must be "self-delighting, self-appeasing, self-affrighting"—affecting a kind of autism of the spirit "though every face should scowl/And every windy quarter howl/Or every bellows burst. . . ."

Yeats's feminine ideal is of course not exclusively his: it is *the* feminine ideal of centuries, the mythic being (or function) of which another poet, Robert Graves, so confidently speaks in declaring: "A woman is a Muse, or she is nothing." What is most unsettling about this sentimental vision is the anger that any "betrayal" arouses in the male. The female is not to concern herself with history, with action; it is her role to simply exist; even her beauty must not be too extreme, so that men will not be disturbed. When Woman fails to conform to this stereotype she is bitterly and savagely denounced: she is "an old bellows full of angry wind." Constance Markiewicz also draws forth the poet's disapproval, in "Easter 1916," for, like Maud Gonne, she has violated masculine expectations:

> That woman's days were spent
> In ignorant good-will
> Her nights in argument
> Until her voice grew shrill.
> What voice more sweet than hers
> When, young and beautiful,
> She rode to harriers?

This crude division between good girl and shrill (hysterical?) woman differs very little from the stereotyping associated with popular or mass culture. But so skillful is Yeats's employment of language that the self-mesmerizing function of his poetry disguises the simplicity of his thought.

Perhaps, too, the poet assumes a masculine privilege by way of his role as a poet, a manipulator of language. For it seems to be a deep-seated prejudice that written language belongs to men, and that any woman who attempts it is violating a natural law. As Thoreau argues with evident reasonableness in the chapter "Reading," in *Walden:*

> Books must be read as deliberately and reservedly as they were written. It is not enough even to be able to speak the language of that nation by which they were written, for there is a memorable interval between the spoken and the written language, the language heard and the language read. The one is commonly transitory, a sound, a tongue, a dialect merely, almost brutish, and we learn it unconsciously, like the brutes, of our mothers. The other is the maturity and experience of that; if that is our mother tongue, this is our father tongue, a reserved and select expression, too significant to be heard by the ear, which we must be born again in order to speak.

If either of our "languages"—spoken or written—is a language of brutes, naturally it will be imagined a Mother Tongue; for the Father Tongue, that "reserved and select expression," necessitates a religious initiation. One must be born again—which is to say, born male.

CAUTIONARY TALES: WOMEN WHO RIDE AWAY

In contrast to Yeats and to what might be called the "genteel" tradition even within Modernism, D. H. Lawrence not only allows women their physical beings but insists upon an immersion in physicality as a redemption from the sterility of the solitary ego. The old, dead, contemptible images of "femininity" are to be destroyed: not for Lawrence the restrictive noble niceness implied by such a title as *The Portrait of a Lady*. Woman's passionate nature is to be celebrated—at least so far as Woman's relationship with Man is concerned.

One of the most compelling aspects of Lawrence's revolutionary art is his attempt, by way of language, to render states of mind—ineffable subtleties of sensual experience and "consciousness"—of a sort that previous writers, with few exceptions, did not approach. Lawrence's contemporary Virginia Woolf argued in a now-famous essay that it is the task of the novelist not to imitate objective life by means of a plot, but to present the "luminous halo" or "semi-transparent envelope" of consciousness as it is experienced inwardly; for Woolf, in the practice of her highly instinctive art, events become no more than small islands in a constantly shifting mental sea. Lawrence, however, clearly wanted to wed the traditional novel with the new: he saw his task as even more challenging, in acknowledging the multifarious influences and impressions that shape the individual from the abstract ("England," religion, tradition) down to the concrete. Lawrence's mental sea is rather more akin to a swift-running river; it rarely turns back upon itself and chokes with an excess of static observations into a sort of prose-poem swamp, as Woolf's writing sometimes does.

What is so disturbing about Lawrence's fiction and poetry, no less than his hectoring essays, is the precision with which his language conveys these shifting, kaleidoscopic states of mind in the service of a dominating (though often unstated) idea. In a sense Lawrence is always preaching; even while rendering dissolution he is always in control. His aim is modest—merely to save our lives, to allow us a second birth. For both men and women, however, this redemption is only possible by way of a baptism in the flesh, in phallic love: the old ego (which is to say, the autonomous personality) must be destroyed. Ursula Brangwen, the defiant heroine of *The Rainbow,* survives a miscarriage and a period of delirium to come to the realization that she should never have a man according to *her* desire: "It was not for her to create, but to recognize a man created by God. The man should come from the Infinite and she should hail him." When, in the succeeding *Women in Love,* Ursula falls in love with Birkin, her first experience is one of the terror of dissolution rather than the euphoria of a more conventional romance:

> As the day wore on, the life-blood seemed to ebb away from Ursula, and in the emptiness a heavy despair gathered. Her passion seemed to bleed to death, and there was nothing. She sat

suspended in a state of complete nullity, harder to bear than death.

"Unless something happens," she said to herself, in the perfect lucidity of final suffering, "I shall die. I am at the end of my line of life." She sat crushed and obliterated in a darkness that was the border of death. . . .[13]

Lawrence meticulously renders the ego's panic at the prospect of its own disintegration. Ursula is not really dying but she is "dying into another" and being expelled from the world of routine and mechanical activity which engages, in Lawrence's view, most people. Passionate erotic love is not altogether human for, as we have seen, it hails from the Infinite: Birkin is both a son of man and a son of God—the bearer, in short, of extraordinary powers. When he next sees Ursula she is in a kind of trance. "He looked at her and wondered at the luminous delicacy of her beauty, and the wide shining of her eyes. He watched from a distance, with wonder in his heart; she seemed transfigured with light." Male and female are eventually bound together by a sensual and sexual love they cannot control; Ursula and Birkin marry. In their primary natures—in Ursula's *femaleness*, Birkin's *maleness*—they are fulfilled, however mercurial and combative they continue to be in more superficial respects.

Ursula's younger sister Gudrun is by far the more interesting of the sisters. Like Ursula she is high-spirited, independent, and unafraid of passion; but she is an artist as well—a serious artist. So few and so generally unsatisfactory are portraits of women as serious artists (for one cannot grant Virginia Woolf's anemic Lily Briscoe the respect Woolf seems to expect), that Lawrence's complex presentation of Gudrun is all the more valuable. Gudrun's character is certainly based on Katherine Mansfield, with whom Lawrence was closely acquainted; though it is probably more accurate to say that it is based upon Lawrence's highly subjective and prejudiced vision of Mansfield, in which much of himself—his aggression, his egoism, his consumptive ill-health—was projected. (Biographers of both Lawrence and Mansfield take note of an alleged letter Lawrence wrote to Mansfield in 1920, breaking off his friendship with her and John Middleton Murry after Murry had rejected a story of his for the

Athenaeum. Lawrence evidently told Mansfield that he loathed her and hoped she would die, "stewing in [her] consumption." The letter was destroyed by Murry but a number of persons seem to have read it.)[14]

While Ursula comes dangerously close, as a fictitious character, to an assemblage of fluid states of mind, glorying in her physicality, Gudrun is all control: "Life doesn't *really* matter," she says. "It is one's art which is central." Gudrun resists "blood-consciousness" because it terrifies and disgusts her; she feels only repugnance for marriage and the possibility of having children. Named for a mythical Germanic heroine who killed her second husband, Gudrun is the apotheosis of the castrating female, and it is clear that Lawrence is fascinated by her as well as revulsed. She is the autonomous, self-determined, unsentimental female—and a serious and talented artist as well. Gudrun must be represented by Lawrence as unnatural because in his cosmology (as in the cosmology of many men) she is a force beyond "nature." And a competing artist as well.

Gudrun is allowed her angry denunciation of the past, and of middle-class English life in particular, because this is Lawrence's position as well; both he and Gudrun are savagely witty at the expense of the Victorian "religion" of home and family. But Gudrun has no wish to fulfill herself in erotic love. She strikes Gerald precisely because he attracts her so powerfully, and she detests weakness in herself; after he has become her lover she feels herself "destroyed" into consciousness. ("And of what was she conscious?" Gudrun asks herself bitterly. Only the ache of nausea for herself and for her lover, who sleeps unknowing beside her, with a "warm, expressionless beauty.") Where Ursula's ego is broken by way of passionate erotic love, Gudrun's is curiously strengthened, hardened, isolated. She feels herself a monster of consciousness, exulting in what Lawrence has elsewhere called a "rottenness" of the will.

Gudrun, the artist, wants to refashion all the world in the shape of *her* desire. She sees people as characters in books or marionettes in a theater. She dissects them to reduce them to their elements, "to place them in their true light." Her work is miniatures, perfect, exquisite, finished; she would like to see the world "through the wrong end of the opera glasses"; unsurprisingly, she would like to have been born a man. It is Gudrun, and not Hermione, or any other woman in *Women in Love,* who suggests the mythical figure of Aphrodite of whom Birkin speaks: Aphrodite, the flowering mystery of the "death-process," the blood of "destructive creation."

Gudrun's seductiveness is all the more perverse in that it promises no surrender, no fulfillment. She sees a woman's lover as her enemy, to be embraced with her body until she has him "all in her hands, . . . strained into her knowledge." Lawrence's portrait of the female-as-artist is the more powerful because one senses how much of himself he has written into Gudrun: where Lawrence hates, there one is likely to find him: "she wished she were God, to use [Gerald] as a tool." Elsewhere, in his poetry in particular, Lawrence has written of the terrifying near-madness of solipsism, the claustrophobia of the artist who must get the world into his head. That Gudrun is both an artist and a woman is finally intolerable. She must be made to loathe herself, as Lawrence's demonic double. "How I *hate* life, how I hate it!" this talented young woman is made to exclaim.

> There she was, placed before the clock-face of life. And if she turned . . . still she could see, with her very spine, she could see the clock, always the great white clock-face. She knew she was not *really* reading. She was not *really* working. She was watching the fingers twitch across the eternal, mechanical, monotonous clock-face of time. She never really lived, she only watched. Indeed, she was like a little, twelve-hour clock, vis-à-vis with the enormous clock of eternity.[15]

—an image of such potent hellishness, one feels Lawrence is transcribing his own nightmare visions, at white heat.

By contrast we have Connie Chatterly, the "ruddy, country-looking girl with the soft brown hair and sturdy body, and slow movements, full of unusual energy." Though corrupted for a while by the malevolent, overly mental spirit of the times, Connie is a man's woman, a woman only by way of a man: the trajectory of her love affair and her redemption through Mellors, her husband's game-keeper, is too well-known to necessitate analysis. Lady Chatterly has no pretensions of being an artist of any kind. (Compare Lord Chatterly, who dabbles in fiction—satirical, superficial, trifling short pieces.) She surrenders to Mellors and to her own sense of destiny; she is pregnant at the novel's end, united in a mystic marriage with her lover.

It is always something of a surprise to discover how puritanical Lawrence is, beyond the revolutionary rhetoric of certain of his pronouncements; how unexamined are his assumptions that Woman exists for Man and for his ceaseless appraisal. Through Mellors Lawrence appears to be taking revenge on women of his acquaintance who have disappointed him. How various the women Mellors has "loved," and how astonishing the ways in which they have failed him:

—There are women who want a man but who don't want sex, only endure it: the Victorian ideal

—There are women who pretend to enjoy sex, and to be passionate: but it's all theatrical

—There are women who are "unnatural" in various ways, requiring lovemaking of unconventional, unspecified sorts

—There are women like Mellors's former wife who are "active"—too active—and seem to have usurped the natural role of the male

—There are frigid women: " . . . the sort that's just dead inside: but dead: and they know it"

Astonishing, says Mellors, how Lesbian women are, "consciously or unconsciously." And it seems to him that *most women are Lesbian,* in fact. ("Do you mind?" Connie asks, rather disingenuously. Mellors replies: "I could kill them. When I'm with a woman who's really Lesbian, I fairly howl in my soul, wanting to kill her.")[16]

Lawrence's gospel of salvation by way of erotic love, liberating in theory, may in fact constitute one more confinement, the more alarming for its being so popularly confused with freedom. His portraits of women who fail to conform to the "natural" ideal espoused by Mellors are instructive: in the novella *The Fox* two young women who live together companionably are soon divided by a young man, who "accidentally" kills the more masculine of the two; in the particularly sadistic "None of That," a woman who is aggressively attracted to a Spanish bullfighter is given by him to his friends, to be gang-raped; the Lesbian Miss Inger of *The Rainbow* is seen as a "poisonous, corrupt woman" who gives off a "marshy, bittersweet corruption . . . sick and unwholesome," though nothing she *does* in the novel is in the slightest way reprehensible.

The most chilling of Lawrence's cautionary portraits of women is that of the "assured" American woman of *The Woman Who Rode Away*. Though this sacrificial female has not violated nature by aspiring to art, or by imagining herself an intellectual, she seems to have aroused Lawrence's loathing because she is a representative of the white race, the "effete white civilization." Like a crudely sketched Emma Bovary, she imagines it is her destiny to leave her husband and children "to wander into the secret haunts of the timeless, mysterious, marvelous Indians" of the Mexican Sierra Madres. She is a patly symbolic thirty-three when she rides alone to the Chilchui Indians, with the message that she is tired of the white god, and wants to "bring her heart" to the Indian god: a sacrifice that turns out to be literally true.

The Woman Who Rode Away is a curiosity in Lawrence's oeuvre, written in such evident haste, with such uncontrolled fury and loathing, that, like numerous passages in *Kangaroo* and *St. Mawr,* it seems to expose the author in the very act of composition. "Talent is a cosmetic," Nietzsche has wittily observed. "What someone *is,* begins to be revealed when his talent abates, when he stops showing what he can *do.*" Primitive in execution, this novella of 1924 comes very near the brink of unintentional comedy, as a stereotyped "white woman" reiterates her desire to "bring her heart" to dark gods, in the form of stereotyped noble savages who see her not as a woman at all, but as "some giant female white ant." Her bloody sacrifice at the hands of their priest symbolizes the waning of one phase of civilization, or so Lawrence argues.

> Her kind of womanhood, intensely personal and individual, was to be obliterated again, and the great primeval symbols were to tower once more over the fallen individual independence of woman. The sharpness and the quivering nervous consciousness of the highly-bred white woman was to be destroyed again, womanhood was to be cast once more into the great stream of impersonal sex and impersonal passion.[17]

Could any parable more bluntly yield its meaning, and its murderous prophecy? And this, from the man who called himself a "priest of love." Like Freud, Lawrence is one of those "liberators" of the twentieth century whose gospel, as applied to and experienced by women, may in fact constitute a more insidious—precisely *because* iconoclastic—imprisonment. Women who ride away ride away not simply to their deaths at the hands of men, but to their just and necessary deaths. It is their fate, their punishment for being "unnatural" in men's eyes.

FAULKNER'S JOHANNA BURDEN: THE SPINSTER AS NYMPHOMANIAC

In American literature of the nineteenth century masculine energies could be discharged in romantically primitive ways: one could "light out for the territory," like Huck; one could retreat a mile or two into the woods to experiment with "life driven into a corner," like the hero of Thoreau's *Walden;* one could thwart the "damp, drizzly November of the soul" by going to sea, like Ishmael ("This is my substitute for pistol and ball"). It is no accident that much of classic American literature is womanless, since Woman implies a personal and social bond, society, civilization—precisely what Man in his romantic discontent with himself wants to escape. Whales of every species are lyrically celebrated in *Moby Dick* while the vague, sketchy "flashbacks" to women have an air of the contrived and the perfunctory. And who among us is not wholeheartedly on Huck's side in his anxiety to escape Aunt Sally and "civilization"? We have all, in Huck's words, been there before.

Twentieth-century fiction written by men often discharges these primitive energies against women. Faulkner's *Light in August,* Richard Wright's *Native Son* (1940), and Norman Mailer's *An American Dream* (1965) center on murders of women by frustrated and romantically "primitive" heroes whose actions are ambiguous rather than clearly reprehensible. The women victims are provocative and, within the worlds evoked by the novelists, would seem to deserve their brutal fates: one feels that the "great primeval symbols," in Lawrence's words, tower once more over the "individual independence" of women. In *Native Son* the psychopathic black Bigger Thomas murders a white girl of "liberal" tendencies who has behaved recklessly with him; in *An American Dream* Mailer's self-conscious hero Rojack murders his wealthy wife and causes the death of another woman with whom he is sexually involved, in a somewhat confused mystical sequence that celebrates the triumph of instinct—a purely masculine instinct. The murders of women who overstep the boundaries of a fairly conventional decency are felt by the reader as sacrificial and instructive: they are not "crimes" in the ordinary sense. A curious puritanism is at work, passing savage judgment on women who attempt to usurp the freedoms traditionally reserved for men.

One of the few distinctive women in Faulkner's many novels is the spinster Johanna Burden, who is murdered by her lover Joe Christmas at the culmination of their sadomasochistic affair. As her name suggests, Johanna is not completely or satisfactorily female; she has the "strength and fortitude of a man," and "mantrained muscles and . . . mantrained habit of thinking." Like Joe she is an outsider in Mississippi: her people were originally Abolitionists from New Hampshire who were willing to give their lives in the antislavery cause. (As Johanna gives her life, in a sense, to the cause of the "nigger" Christmas.) With a grim, unswerving zeal Johanna has taken on the "burden" of helping blacks better themselves by way of education, though the task can only seem hopeless in the context of the South at this time. (" . . . Escape it you cannot. The curse of the black race is God's curse. But the curse of the white race is the black man who will be forever God's chosen own because He once cursed Him."[18])

The solitary, childless descendant of New Englanders, Johanna still speaks with a Northern accent at the age of forty-one, and is despised by her white neighbors as an unwanted and singularly graceless advocate of Negro causes. Even her black neighbors are condescending: "Colored folks around here look after her," a boy says. Her irrevocable—and fatal—mistake with Joe Christmas is to "see" him as black, though many of Joe's energies have gone into asserting what Faulkner calls his black blood. Implicit throughout this long, lurid, splendidly tangled tale is the contrast between the doomed Johanna Burden and the survivor Lena Grove, who gives birth to a son at the novel's melodramatic conclusion. As her name suggests Lena is passive, bovine, and completely female; she possesses those mammalian charms Faulkner has elsewhere celebrated; she may even be of below average intelligence. (Lena anticipates the more maddening and more voluptuous Eula Varner of *The Hamlet*, she whose "entire appearance suggested some symbology out of the old Dionysic times—honey in sunlight and bursting grapes, the writhen bleeding of the crushed fecundated vine beneath the hard rapacious trampling goat-hoof." Eula is outsized, outrageous, a mythical tall-tale heroine whose very presence drives men to distraction: "She might as well still have been a foetus. It was as if only half of her had been born, that mentality and body had somehow become either completely separated or hopelessly involved." As a child of eight Eula gives off an aphrodisiac odor, to the special despair of her brother Jody who imagines he must guard her virginity.[19]

Johanna, by contrast, is not really a woman. Her consciousness is too active, her identity is confused rather than simplified by biology, she is a sister to those problematic women despised by Yeats and Lawrence. The futile ambition of her work in Negro causes, in a region utterly imbued with the fantasy-belief of white supremacy; the recklessness of her involvement with a man whom she does not know; the violation of her long-preserved virginity; the accelerating wildness of her behavior—these factors condemn Johanna to death.

Joe Christmas is alarmed and rather comically shocked by what Faulkner characterizes as the "throes of nymphomania" in Johanna. He begins to fear actual corruption, though it is not clear to what, or from what previous state of purity, he might be corrupted. In the "sewer" of their relationship Joe begins to see himself "as from a distance, like a man being sucked down into a bottomless morass." Joe and Johanna are not, despite the twinness suggested by their names, *natural* mates.

Johanna Burden is one of the most ambiguous characters in Faulkner's fiction. Like Gail Hightower she is clearly meant to function allegorically; like Hightower, she is never convincing as an integrated personality. We view her through Joe Christmas's eyes, we are meant to judge her in terms of Joe's eerily puritanical standards, yet the distinction between male protagonist and male author is often negligible. Both Joe Christmas and Faulkner are bemused, disgusted, fascinated, and finally outraged by this extraordinary woman who is not one but, perhaps, two people: "the one whom [Joe] saw now and then by day and looked at while they spoke to one another with speech that told nothing at all since it didn't try to and didn't intend to; the other with whom he lay at night and didn't see, speak to, at all." Johanna's daytime personality, her very *identity,* is insignificant; it is her night-self, the corrupted flesh, that exerts a deathly fascination. Faulkner's portrait of the spinster as despised nymphomaniac is awkward and crude, yet instructive: for what is "Johanna Burden" but a male projection of particular savagery, the nightmare double that *must* be acknowledged in the (corrupted) flesh, and *must* then be exorcized, with violence if necessary? It cannot be accidental that Joe nearly saws off Johanna's head after murdering her.

After Joe Christmas has been Johanna Burden's lover for a year he still enters her house, and climbs the stairs to her bedroom, like a thief, to despoil her "virginity" each time anew. Their initial mating is blunt, unsentimental, and presumably without emotion, for Johanna has the "unselfpitying" temperament of a man: "There was no feminine vacillation, no coyness of obvious desire and intention to succumb at last. It was as if he struggled physically with another man for an object of no value to either, and for which they struggled on principle alone." But what is the principle? And why is the mating so repulsive? Poor Joe muses:

> "My God . . . it was like I was the woman and she was the man." But that was not right, either. Because she had resisted to the very last. But it was not woman resistance, that resistance which, if really meant, cannot be overcome by any man for the reason that the woman observes no rules of physical combat. But she had resisted fair, by the rules that decreed that upon a certain crisis one was defeated, whether the end of resistance had come or not."[20]

This incidental dismissal of the very possibility of rape in male-female relations goes unremarked. Interesting, too, is the Faulknerian sentiment that in resisting men, women observe no "rules" of physical combat, and that Johanna, by "resisting fair" her attacker, abdicates claims to normal femininity. Raping her a second time Joe Christmas thinks, enraged: "At least I have made a woman of her at last. . . . Now she hates me. I have taught her that, at least."

But Johanna hasn't been taught; Johanna hasn't, evidently, been made a woman. Like her sister-nymphomaniac, Temple Drake of *Sanctuary,*[21] Johanna seems to maintain an unnatural virginity even after repeated assaults. She insults her lover's precarious sense of his own sexuality by keeping intact her *inward autonomy.* These are vicious and even demented sentiments which, if followed to a logical conclusion, would indict the victim for having been the "cause" of the crime. ("I shall never, never forgive the old pawnbroker," Raskolnikov cries, long after he has smashed the old woman's head with the blunt edge of an ax.)

Faulkner's mesmerized repugnance for Johanna Burden springs primarily from his sense of masculine outrage at the woman's forthright and "unfeminine" sexual desire. The portrait of this fictitious spinster-as-nymphomaniac, frankly preposterous in its particulars, clearly answers to a deep-buried terror in the author's psyche, which the amoral and promiscuous Joe Christmas is obliged to express. It is Faulkner, after all, and not the semiliterate Joe, who accuses Johanna of succumbing to such an extreme of nymphomania that she tears her clothing to ribbons awaiting him, "her body gleaming in the slow shifting from one to another of such formally erotic attitudes and gestures as a Beardsley of the time of Petronius might have drawn." This comically grotesque woman has eyes that glow in the dark "like the eyes of cats"; when she reaches for her affrighted lover, each strand of her wild hair "would seem to come alive like octopus tentacles." The degree of her corruption is signaled by her panting cry: "Negro! Negro! Negro!"

In the daytime, the New England spinster wears plain cotton dresses and clean, starched, proper bonnets; only her lover knows that beneath this fraudulent feminine costume lies the "rotten richness ready to flow into putrefaction at a touch, like something growing in a swamp." At the same time Joe is frustrated by the thought that, under her clothes, Johanna "can't even be made so that it could have happened"—by which he means, so that he is himself the male, the aggressor. The bottomless morass he fears is perhaps the male terror of "sinking" into the female, and losing the identity of maleness which is his only claim to an ontological being. If he is not male—if the female does not acknowledge it—does he exist?

If male-female relations in Faulkner constitute an unarticulated struggle in which the defeat of the female is necessary to ensure the male's sense of his very existence, the degree of savagery unleashed against the "unfeminine" Johanna Burden, by both male protagonist and male author, is less surprising. Faulkner so manipulates his characters that Johanna provokes Joe Christmas into murdering her in what might be seen as self-defense, since his concern is to provide his hero with an appropriate catalyst, a guilty cause, for the act of murder. (An act that brings with it an extraordinary punishment— Joe's castration by the fanatic Percy Grimm at the novel's end.) The reader is meant to share Faulkner's irony in the demonstration of popular, indeed traditional, Southern prejudice against blacks, by way of Grimm's remark to the dying Joe Christmas ("Now you'll let white women alone, even in hell"); but the female reader is sensitive to an even more pointed irony—the dead woman at the center of the novel is judged as rightly dead, and her murderer is "innocently" guilty, in the service of a complex of passions that dramatize the tragic relations between white and black *men*. Much in *Light in August* is rushed, overblown, clotted, confused; but the central parable is unmistakably clear, for this, too, is a cautionary tale. Johanna Burden is murdered, Lena Grove gives birth to a son she calls "Joey." It might be said of both women by the novel's end: "At least I have made a woman of her."

The Magnanimity of Wuthering Heights

Once upon a time, it seems, an English clergyman born Brunty or Branty, self-baptized the more romantic Brontë, brought home to his four children a box of twelve wooden soldiers. The children lived in isolation in a parsonage high on the Yorkshire moors, which is to say, at the edge of the world; each was possessed of an extraordinarily fecund imagination; the wooden soldiers soon acquired life and identities (among them the Duke of Wellington and Bonaparte). The way by which a masterpiece as unanticipated as *Wuthering Heights* comes to be written, involving, as it did, the gradual evolution from such early childish games to more complex games of written language (serial stories transcribed by the children in minute italic handwriting meant to resemble print; secret plays, or "bed plays," written at bedtime; the transcribing of the ambitious Gondal and Angria sagas, which were to be viable for nearly fifteen years) is so compelling a tale, so irresistible a legend, one is tempted to see in it a miniature history of the imagination's triumph, in the most socially restricted of environments. No poet or novelist would wish to reduce his mature works to the status of mere games, or even to acknowledge an explicit kinship with the prodigies of the child's dreaming mind; but it is clear that the play of the imagination has much to do with childish origins, and may, in truth, be inseparable from it. As Henry James has observed, in a somewhat peevish aside regarding the "romantic tradition" and the "public ecstasies" surrounding the Brontë sisters, "Literature is an objective, a projected result; it is life that is the unconscious, the agitated, the struggling, floundering cause." Certainly this is true, but its dogma is too blunt, too assured, to inspire absolute confidence. The unconscious energies feed the objective project; life fuels art, in disguised forms, though art is, of course, a highly conscious activity. Literature is far more than a game of words, a game ingeniously constructed *of* words, but the imagination is expansive enough to accommodate both the child's fantasies and the stratagems of the adult. Out of that long-lost box of wooden soldiers, or its forgotten equivalent, we have all sprung.

It is not simply in contrast to its origins that *Wuthering Heights* strikes us as so unique, so unanticipated. This great novel, though not inordinately long, and, contrary to general assumption, not inordinately complicated, manages to be a number of things: a romance that brilliantly challenges the basic presumptions of the "romantic"; a "gothic" that evolves—with an absolutely inevitable grace—into its temperamental opposite; a parable of innocence and loss, and childhood's necessary defeat; and a work of consummate skill on its primary level, that is, the level of language. Above all, it is a history: its first statement is the date 1801; and one of its final statements involves New Year's Day (of 1803). It seeks both to dramatize and to explain how the ancient stock of the Earnshaws are restored to their rights (the somber house of Wuthering Heights, built in 1500), and, at the same time, how and why the last of the Earnshaws, Hareton, will be leaving the Heights to live, with his cousin-bride, at Thrushcross Grange. One generation has given way to the next: the primitive energies of childhood have given way to the intelligent compromises of adulthood. The history of the Earnshaws and the Lintons begins to seem a history, writ small, albeit with exquisite detail, of civilization itself.

As a historical novel, published in 1847, "narrated" by Lockwood in 1801–1802, and encompassing an interior story that begins in the late summer of 1771, *Wuthering Heights* is expansive enough to present two overlapping and starkly contrasting tales: the first, and more famous, a somewhat lurid tragedy of betrayal erected upon a fantasy of childhood (or incestuous) "romance"; the second, a story of education, maturing, and accommodation to the exigencies of time. Both stories partake of the slightly fabulous, especially the first (in which, with fairy-tale inevitability, a "gypsy" foundling, named for a dead son, usurps a father's love); both seem to progress less as a consequence of individual and personal desire than of the abstract (and predetermined) evolution of "Nature" into "Society." The great theme of *Wuthering Heights,* perversely overlooked by many of its admiring critics, as well as by its detractors, is precisely this *inevitability:* how present-day harmony, in September of 1802, has come about. Far from being a rhapsodical ode to primitive dark energies, populated by savages (whether noble or otherwise), the novel is, in fact, as its elaborate structure makes clear, an assured demonstration of the finite and tragically self-consuming nature of "passion." Romantic and gothic elements cannot survive in the sunlit world of sanity (as Lockwood jealously observes, the second Catherine and her fiancé Hareton look as if, together, "they would brave Satan and all his legions"); the new generation will settle in the more commodious Thrushcross Grange, opening, as it does, in symbolic and literal terms, onto the rest of the world. The curious spell or curse has lifted from the principals of the drama, and will continue to hold sway—so local rumor will have it, doubtless for centuries—only on the moors, where the redoubtable Heathcliff and a woman yet walk, on every rainy night. ("Idle tales," says Mrs. Dean, "and so say I." The city-bred Lockwood concurs, and we are invited, however ambiguously, to concur, in the history's closing remark, as Lockwood wonders "how any one could ever imagine unquiet slumbers for the sleepers in that quiet earth.")

A novel's strategy reveals itself in structure and process, not in isolated passages or speeches, however striking. Any complex work that aspires to a statement about something larger than the experiences it depicts must be understood as a proposition on two levels: that of the immediate, or present time (the shared fiction of the "immediate" as it is evidently experienced by both participant and reader, simultaneously), and that of the historical (in which the fiction of the simultaneous experience of participant and reader is dissolved, and the reader emerges, ideally, at least, with a god's-eye view of the novelist's design). The playful braiding of narrators and magisterial creator that is so pronounced a characteristic of Nabokov's novels is perhaps more willfully ingenious than the "Chinese box" narration of Emily Brontë (which, one should hasten to say, she chose to employ, as a felicitous convention, and did not invent), but scarcely more effective. As much as any Modernist work, *Wuthering Heights* demands to be reread: the first three chapters (charting the disingenuous Lockwood's introduction to the surly enigmatic inhabitants of Wuthering Heights, both living and dead) yield the author's intention *only* upon a second reading. And this has not only to do with the time-honored device of withheld information, but with the reader's literal interpretation of Lockwood's experience: for Lockwood is himself a "reader," albeit a most confused one, in these initial chapters.

It is on the level of visceral immediacy, as a fictional "world" is evoked through the employment of language, that a novel lives or dies, or struggles along in a sort of twilit sleep; it is on this higher level, where structure and design are grasped, and all novels make claim to be "histories" (the eager demands of *how* and *why,* as well as *what,* accommodated), that it acquires a more cultural or generalized value. Emily Brontë's sense of the parable residing beneath her melodramatic tale guides us throughout: for we are allowed to know, despite the passionate and painfully convincing nostalgia for the

Heights, the moors, and childhood, evinced by Catherine and Heathcliff, that their values, and hence their world (the Heights) are doomed. We acquiesce rather to the lyricism of the text, than to its actual claims: the triumph of the second Catherine and Hareton (the "second" Heathcliff), not only in their union but in their proposed move away from the ancient home of the Earnshaws, is a triumph that quite refutes traditional readings of the novel that dwell upon its dark, brooding, unconscious, and even savage energies. Meaning in literature cannot of course reside solely in the apprehension of design, for one might argue that "meaning" is present in every paragraph, every sentence, every word; but for the novelist such elements as scenes of a dramatic nature, description, historical background, summary of action, etc., are subordinate to the larger, grander, more spacious structure. If *Wuthering Heights* is the title of this phase of "our" collective history, ending on New Year's Day of 1803, *Thrushcross Grange* will be the title of the next.

Who will inherit the earth's riches? Who will inherit a stable, rather than a self-consuming, love? What endures, for mankind's sake, is not the violent and narcissistic love of Catherine and Heathcliff (who identify with each other, as fatal twins, rather than individuals), but the easier, more friendly, and altogether more plausible love of the second Catherine and Hareton Earnshaw. How ironic, then, that Brontë's brilliantly imagined dialectic, arguing for the *inevitable* exorcism of the old demons of childhood, and professing an attitude toward time and change that might even be called optimistic, should have been, and continues to be, misread. That professional critics identify subject matter in *process* with an ambitious novel's *design* is one of the curiosities of literary history, and bears an uncomfortable resemblance to the myopic activities of the self-appointed censor, who judges a book by a certain word, on page 58 or 339, and has no need to trouble himself with the rest. *Wuthering Heights* is no less orderly and ritualistic a work than a representative Greek tragedy, or a novel of Jane Austen's, though its author's concerns are with disorderly and even chaotic elements. One of the wonders of the novel is its astonishing magnanimity, for all the clichés of Emily Brontë's "narrowness." Where else might we find a tough-minded lyricism evoking the mystical value of Nature, contiguous with a vision of the possibilities of erotic experience very like that of the Decadents, or of Sade himself? Where else might we find passionate soliloquies and self-lacerations, of a Dostoyevskian quality, housed in utterly homely, and fastidiously rendered, surroundings? Both Brontë and Melville draw upon Shakespeare for the speeches of certain of their principals (Heathcliff being, in the remarkable concluding pages of the novel, as succinctly eloquent as Edmund, Iago, Macbeth), but it is Brontë's novel that avoids the unnatural strain of allegory, and gives a local habitation to outsized passions.

Wuthering Heights is erected upon not only the accumulated tensions and part-formed characters of adolescent fantasy (adumbrated in the Gondal sagas) but upon the very theme of adolescent, or even childish, or infantile, fantasy. In the famous and unfailingly moving early scene in which Catherine Earnshaw tries to get into Lockwood's chamber (more specifically her old oak-paneled bed, in which, nearly a quarter of a century earlier, she and the child Heathcliff customarily slept together), it is significant that she identifies herself as *Catherine Linton* though she is in fact a child; and that she informs Lockwood that she had lost her way on the moor, for twenty years. As Catherine Linton, married, and even pregnant, she has never been anything other than a child: this is the pathos of her situation, and not the fact that she wrongly, or even rightly, chose to marry Edgar Linton over Heathcliff. Brontë's emotions are clearly caught up with these child's predilections, as the evidence of her poetry reveals, but the greatness of her genius as a novelist allows her a magnanimity, an imaginative elasticity, that challenges the very premises (which aspire to philosophical detachment) of the Romantic exaltation of the child and childhood's innocence.

The highly passionate relationship between Catherine and Heathcliff, forged in their embittered and savage childhood, has been variously interpreted: it is a doomed "gothic" romance, whose depth of feeling makes the inane Lockwood and his narrative-mate Mrs. Dean appear all the more shallow; it is curiously chaste, for all its emotional outpourings, and as finally "innocent" as any love between sister and brother; then again, it is rude, lurid, unwholesome, intensely erotic, and suggestive of an incestuous bond—indeed. Heathcliff is named for a dead brother of Catherine's, and he, Hindley, and Catherine have slept together as children. (The reasons for Mr. Earnshaw's adoption of the gypsy waif, the goblin, the parentless demon, the dark-skinned "cuckoo," are never made plausible within the story; but it is perhaps instructive to learn that Emily Brontë's great-great-grandfather Hugh Brunty had adopted a black-haired foundling from Liverpool—who in turn adopted their own grandfather, the younger Hugh. So the vertiginous interrelations and mirror-selves of the novel's central household have, for all their fairy-tale implausibility, an ancestral authenticity.)

So famous are certain speeches in *Wuthering Heights* proclaiming Catherine's bond with Heathcliff ("Nelly, I *am* Heathcliff—he's always, always in my mind"),[1] and Heathcliff's with Catherine ("Oh, God! it is unutterable! I *cannot* live without my life! I *cannot* live without my soul!")[2] that they scarcely require reference, at any length: the peculiarity in the lovers' feeling for each other being their intense and unshakable identification, which is an identification with the moors, and with Nature itself, that seems to preclude any human, let alone "sexual" bond. They do not behave like adulterous lovers, but speak freely of their relationship before Catherine's husband, Edgar; and they embrace, desperately and fatally, in the presence of the ubiquitous and somewhat voyeuristic Mrs. Dean. (Mrs. Dean is even present, in a sense, when, many years later, Heathcliff bribes the sexton to unearth Catherine's coffin, so that he can embrace her mummified corpse, and dream of "dissolving with her, and being more happy still.") So intense an identification between lover and beloved has nothing to do with the dramatic relationship of opposites, who yearn to come together in order to be complete: it is the at-one-ness of the mystic with his God, the peaceful solitude of the unborn babe in the womb. That Heathcliff's prolonged love for the dead Catherine shades by degrees into actual madness is signaled by his breakdown at the novel's conclusion, when the "monomania" for his idol becomes a monomania for death. She, the beloved, implored to return to haunt him, has returned in a terrifying and malevolent way, and will not give him peace. ". . . For what is not connected with her to me? and what does not recall her? I cannot look down to this floor, but her features are shaped in the flags! In every cloud, in every tree—filling the air at night, and caught by glimpses in every object by day—I am surrounded with her image! The most ordinary faces of men and women—my own features—mock me with a resemblance."[3] So Heathcliff tries to explain the frightening "change" that is upon him, when he sees that he and Catherine have been duplicated, in a sense, and supplanted, by the second Catherine and young Hareton. The old energies of the child's untrammeled life have passed over into the ghoulish energies of death, to which Heathcliff succumbs by degrees. "I have to remind myself to breathe—almost to remind my heart to beat!" Heathcliff, that most physical of beings, declares. "And it is like bending back a stiff spring; it is by compulsion that I do the slightest act not prompted by one thought, and by compulsion, that I notice anything alive, or dead, which is not associated with one universal idea. . . . I am swallowed up in the anticipation of its fulfillment."[4]

So far as the romantic plot is concerned, it is Catherine's decision to enter into a misguided engagement with Edgar Linton that precipitates the tragedy: more specifically, a melodramatic accident by which Heathcliff overhears part of Catherine's declaration to Mrs. Dean, but creeps away in shame before he can hear her avowal of abiding love for *him*. In truth, however, the "tragedy" has very little to do with Catherine's conscious will, but seems to have sprung from a phenomenon so impersonal as the passage of time itself. How exquisite, because irremediable, the anguish of "growing up"! Brontë's first-generation lovers would share a kingdom on the moors as timeless, and as phantasmal, as any imagined by Poe. In place of Poe's androgynous male lovers we have the immature Heathcliff (only twenty years old when Catherine dies); in place of the vampire

Ligeia, or the amenorrheic Lady Madeleine, is the tomboyish Catherine, whose life has become a terrifying "blank" since the onset of puberty. No more poignant words have been written on the baffled anguish of the child-self, propelled into an unwanted maturity, and accursed by a centripetal force as pitiless as the north wind that blows upon the Heights. Catherine, though pregnant, and soon to give birth, has absolutely no consciousness of the life in her womb, which belongs to the unimagined future and will become, in fact, the "second" Catherine: she is all self, only self, so arrested in childhood that she cannot recognize her own altered face in the mirror. Brontë's genius consists in giving an unforgettable voice to this seductive and deathly centripetal force we all carry within us:

> I thought . . . that I was enclosed in the oak-panelled bed at home; and my heart ached with some great grief which, just waking, I could not recollect. I pondered, and worried myself to discover what it could be, and, most strangely, the whole past seven years of my life grew a blank! I did not recall that they had been at all. I was a child; my father was just buried, and my misery arose from the separation that Hindley had ordered between me and Heathcliff. I was laid alone, for the first time, and, rousing from a dismal doze after a night of weeping, I lifted my hand to push the panels aside. . . . I cannot say why I felt so wildly wretched . . . I wish I were a girl again, half savage, and hardy, and free; and laughing at injuries, not maddening under them! Why am I so changed? Why does my blood rush into a hell of tumult at a few words? I'm sure I should be myself were I once among the heather on those hills.[5]

Why the presumably robust Catherine Earnshaw's life should end, in a sense, at the age of twelve; why, as a married woman of nineteen, she should know herself irrevocably "changed"—the novel does not presume to explain. This *is* the substance of tragedy, the hell of tumult that is character and fate combined. Her passion for Heathcliff notwithstanding, Catherine's identification is with the frozen and peopleless void of an irrecoverable past, and not with anything human. The feathers she pulls out of her pillow are of course the feathers of dead, wild birds, moorcocks and lapwings: they compel her to think not of the exuberance of childhood, but of death, and even premature death, which is associated with her companion Heathcliff. (Since Heathcliff had set a trap over the lapwing's nest, the mother dared not return, and "we saw its nest in the winter, full of little skeletons.")

This bleak, somber, deathly wisdom is as memorably expressed by Sylvia Plath in her poem "Wuthering Heights," with its character-istic images of a dissolving landscape opening upon the void. Plath, like the fictitious Catherine, suffered a stubborn and irrevocable loss in childhood, and her recognition of the precise nature of this loss is expressed in a depersonalized vocabulary. How seductive, how chill, how terrifying Brontë's beloved moor!

> There is no life higher than the grasstops
> Or the hearts of sheep, and the wind
> Pours by like destiny, bending
> Everything in one direction.
> I can feel it trying
> To funnel my heat away.
> If I pay the roots of the heather
> Too close attention, they will invite me
> To whiten my bones among them.[6]

It is to the roots of the heather that Catherine has paid her fiercest attention.

The novel's second movement, less dramatically focused, but no less rich in observed and often witty detail, transcribes the gradual metamorphosis of the "gothic romance" into its approximate oppo-site. The abandoned and brutish child Hareton, once discovered in the act of hanging puppies from a chair-back, matures into a good-hearted youth who aids the second Catherine in planting flowers in a forbidden "garden"—and becomes her protector at the Heights. Where all marriages were blighted, and two most perversely (the marriages between Heathcliff and Isabella, and the second Catherine and Heathcliff's son Linton), a marriage of emblematic significance will be celebrated. Everyone will leave the Heights, save the comi-

cally embittered old Joseph, the very spirit of sour, gnarled, unchari-
table Christianity, who presumably cannot die.

How this miraculous transformation comes about, *why* it must
be grasped as inevitable, has to do with the novelist's grasp of a
cyclical timelessness beneath the melodramatic action. The rhythm of
the narrative is systaltic, by which I mean not only the strophe and
antistrophe of the sudden cuts back to Lockwood in Mrs. Dean's
presence, and alone (musing in his diary) but also the subtle
counterpoint between the poetic and theatrical speeches of the
principal characters, and the life of the Heights with its harvests and
apple-pickings and hearths that must be swept clean, its tenant
farmers, its vividly observed and felt *reality*. The canny physicality of
Wuthering Heights distinguishes it at once from the "gothic," and
from Shakespeare's tragedies as well, where we are presented with an
exorcism of evil and an implied (but often ritualistic) survival of
good, but never *really* convinced that this survival is a genuine and
not merely a thematic possibility.

Heathcliff, who is said never to read books, comments scornfully
on the fact that his young bride Isabella had pictured in him a hero of
romance. So wildly deluded was this sheltered daughter of
Thrushcross Grange, she expected chivalrous devotion to her, and
"unlimited indulgences." Heathcliff's mockery makes us aware of our
own bookish expectations of him, for he is defiantly *not* a hero, and
we are warned to avoid Isabella's error in "forming a fabulous notion
of my character." Brontë's wit in this passage is supreme, for she
allows her "hero" to define himself in opposition to a gothic-
romantic stereotype she suspects her readers (well into the twentieth
century) cherish; and she allows him, by way of ridiculing poor
masochistic Isabella, to ridicule such readers as well.

> Are you sure you hate me? If I let you alone for half a day, won't
> you come sighing and wheedling to me again? . . . The first thing
> she saw me do, on coming out of the Grange, was to hang up her
> little dog; and when she pleaded for it the first words I uttered
> were a wish that I had the hanging of every being belonging to
> her, except one: possibly she took that exception for herself. But

no brutality disgusted her: I suppose she has an innate admiration of it, if only her precious person were secure from injury! Now, was it not the depth of absurdity—of genuine idiocy—for that pitiful, slavish, mean-minded brach to dream that I could love her? . . . I never, in all my life, met with such an abject thing as she is. She even disgraces the name of Linton; and I've sometimes relented, from pure lack of invention, in my experiments on what she could endure, and still creep shamefully cringing back![7]

This, in Isabella's presence; and naturally Isabella is pregnant. But then Heathcliff observes, in an aside, that he, too, is caught up in this relentless "moral teething," and seems incapable of feeling pity for his victims or for himself. "The more the worms writhe, the more I yearn to crush out their entrails!" he says. " . . . And I grind with greater energy, in proportion to the increase of pain."[8] He observes elsewhere that the mere sight of cowering, weak, fearful persons awakens the desire in him to hurt; and an evening's "slow vivisection" of his own son and his child-bride Catherine would amuse him. Even the elder Catherine, who recognizes her kinship with him, calls him a cruel, wolfish man; and she, of all the persons who know him, understands that he is beyond redemption—precisely because he is not a character in a romantic novel, or, indeed, answerable to any "fabulous notions" at all. (If he weakens at the novel's end, it is only physically. His forthright judgment on his actions is: " . . . As to repenting of my injustices, I've done no injustice, and I repent of nothing—I'm too happy, and yet I'm not happy enough.")

Heathcliff's enduring appeal is approximately that of Edmund, Iago, Richard III, the intermittent Macbeth: the villain who impresses by way of his energy, his cleverness, his peculiar sort of courage; and by his asides, inviting, as they do, the audience's or reader's collaboration in wickedness. Brontë is perfectly accurate in having her villain tell us, by way of Mrs. Dean and Lockwood, that brutality does not always disgust; and that there are those persons—often of weak, cringing, undeveloped character—who "innately admire" it, provided they themselves are not injured. (Though, in Isabella's case, it would seem that she has enjoyed, and even provoked, her husband's "experimental" sadism.) Heathcliff presides over a veritable cornucopia of darksome episodes: he beats and kicks the fallen Hindley, he throws a knife at Isabella, he savagely slaps young Catherine, he doesn't trouble to summon a doctor for his dying son, as he no longer has any use for him. Unfailingly cruel, yet sly enough to appear exasperated with his victims' testing of his cruelty, Heathcliff arouses the reader to this peculiar collaborative bond by the sheer force of his language, and his wit: for is he not, with his beloved gone, the lifeforce gone wild? He has no opposition worthy of him; he has no natural mate remaining; he is characterless and depersonalized will—a masklike grimace that can never relax into a smile. (Significantly, Heathcliff is grinning as a corpse—"grinning at death" as old Joseph notes.) Very few readers of *Wuthering Heights* have cared to observe that there is no necessary or even probable connection between the devoted lover of Catherine, and the devoted hater of all the remaining world (including—and this most improbably—Catherine's own daughter Catherine, who resembles her): for certain stereotypes persist so stubbornly they may very well be archetypes, evoking, as they do, an involuntary identification with energy, evil, will, *action*. The mass murderer who is really tender-hearted, the rapist whose victims provoke him, the Führer who is a vegetarian and in any case loves dogs. . . . Our anxieties, which may well spring from childhood experiences, have much to do with denying the *actual* physicality of the outrages, whether those of Heathcliff or any villian, literary or historic, and supplanting for them, however magically, however pitiably, "spiritual" values. If Heathcliff grinds his victims beneath his feet like worms, is it not natural to imagine that they *are* worms, and deserve their suffering, is it not natural to imagine that they are not us? We feel only contempt for the potential sadist Linton, who sucks on sugar candy, and whose relationship with his child-wife parodies a normal love relationship (he asks her not to kiss him, because it makes him breathless). Consequently our temptation is to align ourselves with Heathcliff, as Brontë shrewdly understands. Heathcliff pricks the reader's Linton-like imagination in such passages:

I was embarrassed how to punish him, when I discovered his part in the business—he's such a cobweb, a pinch would annihilate him, but you'll see by his look that he has received his due! I brought him down one evening . . . and just set him in a chair, and never touched him afterwards. I sent Hareton out, and we had the room to ourselves. In two hours, I called Joseph to carry him up again; and, since then, my presence is as potent on his nerves as a ghost; and I fancy he sees me often, though I am not near. Hareton says he wakes and shrieks in the night by the hour together. . . .[9]

Yet the novel is saturated with gothic episodes and images, as many critics have noted, and the tone of motiveless cruelty that prevails, in the opening chapters, clearly has nothing to do with the mature Heathcliff's "plan for revenge." The presumably good-hearted and maternal Mrs. Dean tells Heathcliff that since he is taller than Edgar Linton, and twice as broad across the shoulders, he could "knock him down in a twinkling"—whereupon the boy's face brightens for a moment. The presumably genteel Lintons of Thrushcross Grange are not upset that their bulldog Skulker has caught a little girl by the ankle, and that she is bleeding badly; they evince alarmed surprise only when they learn that the child is Miss Earnshaw, of Wuthering Heights. (As for the child Heathcliff: ". . . The villain scowls so plainly in his face: would it not be a kindness to the country to hang him at once, before he shows his nature in acts, as well as features?")[10] One of the most puzzling revelations in the early section is that, after Mr. Earnshaw has gone to the trouble of bringing the foundling home, his own wife's wish is to "fling it out of doors"; and Mrs. Dean places "it" on the landing with the hope that "it might be gone on the morrow"—though where the luckless creature might go in this wild landscape, one would be hard pressed to say. Clearly we are in a gothic world contiguous with Lear's, where daughters turn their fathers out into the storm, and blinded men are invited to sniff their way to safety.

This combative atmosphere is the natural and unspoiled Eden for which the dying Catherine yearns, however inhuman it is. For, like Heathcliff, she is an "exile" and "outcast" elsewhere: only the primitive and amoral child's world can accommodate her stunted character, until she is reborn and transmogrified in a Catherine part-Earnshaw and part-Linton.

As for Heathcliff, with his diabolical brow and basilisk eyes, his cannibal teeth, his desperate passion for revenge, is he not a "romantic" incarnation of Iago or Vendice (of *The Revenger's Tragedy*), another Edmund fired to destroy an Edgar, a revenge-motive imposed upon a fairy tale of love and betrayal? He does not require Hindley to flog and beat him, in order to turn stoically wicked, since he has possessed an implacable will from the very first, having demonstrated no affection or gratitude for the elder Mr. Earnshaw, who had not only saved his life in Liverpool but (for reasons not at all clear in realistic terms) had loved him above his own children. Near the end of the novel Mrs. Dean wonders aloud if her master might be a ghoul or a vampire, since he has begun to prowl the moor at night, and she has read of "such hideous, incarnate demons." Her characteristic common sense wavers; she sinks into sleep, taxing herself with the rhetorical question: "But where did he come from, the little dark thing, harboured by a good man to his bane?"—a question that is presumably ours as well. From where does "evil" spring, after all, if not from "good"? And is it sired by "good"? And "harboured" by it? This particular demon is Heathcliff only: Heathcliff Heathcliff, possessing no other name: sired, it would seem, by himself, and never legally adopted by Mr. Earnshaw. (His headstone reads only "Heathcliff" and the date of his death: no one can think of an appropriate inscription for his monument.)

Yet if Heathcliff must enact the depersonalized role of a damned spirit, the "romantic" motif of the novel necessitates his having been a victim himself—not of Hindley or of the "ruling classes," but of his soul-mate Catherine. He is unkillable but may die from within, willing his own extinction, as his "soul's bliss kills his body, but does not satisfiy itself." Just as the narcissistic self-laceration of the child-lovers cannot yield to so social and communal a ritual as marriage, so, too, does the "romantic-gothic" mode consume itself, and retreat into history: for the fiction of *Wuthering Heights* must be that we have had Lockwood's diary put into our hands, many years after his transcription of events belonging to another century. We read his "reading" of Mrs. Dean's tale, parts of which seem remote and even legendary. Ghosts are by popular tradition trapped on an earthly plane, cursed by the need, which any compulsive-obsessive neurotic might understand, to cross and recross the same unyielding terrain, never advancing, never progressing, never attaining the freedom of adulthood. Even Edgar, the wronged husband, the master of Thrushcross Grange, soliloquizes:

> I've prayed often . . . for the approach of what is coming: and now I begin to shrink, and fear it. I thought the memory of the hour I came down that glen a bridegroom would be less sweet than the anticipation that I was soon, in a few months, or, possibly, weeks, to be carried up, and laid in its lonely hollow! Ellen, I've been very happy with my little Cathy. . . . But I've been as happy musing by myself among those stones, under that old church, lying, through the long June evenings, on the green mound of her mother's grave, and wishing—yearning for the time when I might lie beneath it.[11]

Considering his late wife's vehement rejection of him, this is an extraordinary statement, and Edgar goes on to say that, to prevent Heathcliff's victimization of his daughter, he would "rather resign her to God, and lay her in the earth before me." Nothing is learned in the older generation; the ease of death is preferred to the combat of life. The wonder is that so strong-willed a personality as young Catherine can have sprung from such debilitated soil.

So with the perpetual childhood of myths, fairy tales, legends, and gothic romances, which, occupying a timeless "present," relate to no time at all. Being outsized and exemplary of passions, their characters cannot be human: they are frozen in a single attitude, they *are* an attitude, and can never develop. Only young Catherine undergoes a change of personality, and, in willfully altering her own fate, transforms the Heights itself. She alone resists Heathcliff; she nurses her invalid husband in his final sickness, and nearly succumbs to death herself. When Heathcliff somewhat uncharacteristically asks her how she feels, after Linton has died, she says: "He's safe, and I'm free. . . . I should feel well—but . . . you have left me so long to struggle against death alone, that I feel and see only death! I feel like death!"[12]—a speech that allows us to see how very far Catherine has come, within a remarkably brief span of time.

In another sort of novel Heathcliff would assuredly have been drawn to his widowed daughter-in-law, if only for sexual, or exploitative purposes: but *Wuthering Heights* is fiercely chaste, and none of its characters gives any impression of being violated by a sexual idea. (The fact that Catherine is pregnant, and that her pregnancy is advanced, during the final tempestuous love scene between her and Heathcliff, is never commented upon by anyone: not even by the unequivocal Mrs. Dean, whose domain is the physical world and whose eye is presumably undimmed by romance. One must be forgiven for wondering if the pregnancy—the incontestably huge belly of Catherine Linton—is not acknowledged because it is so blatant a fact of physical life, so absolute a fact of her *wifehood*, which excludes Heathcliff; or because, given the Victorian strictures governing author as well as characters, it cannot be acknowledged. Perhaps there is simply no vocabulary to enclose it.)

Young Catherine, however, has not inherited her mother's predilection for the grave. She soon exhibits an altogether welcome instinct for self-knowledge and compromise—for the subtle stratagems of adult life—that have been, all along, absent in her elders. Where Heathcliff by his nature remains fixed and two-dimensional, a character in a bygone drama, until his final "change" draws him so unresistingly to death, Catherine's nature is bound up with, and enforced by, the cyclical motion of the seasons: her triumph over him is therefore inevitable. Once or twice she lapses to the self-absorbed manner of the elder Catherine, in seeking (futilely) to provoke two men into fighting over her; but she is too clever to persist. That she learns to accommodate Hareton's filial affection for his monstrous "father" indicates the scope and range of her new maturity—an attribute, it must be said, that genuinely surprises the reader. For suddenly it becomes possible at Wuthering Heights, as if for the first time in human history, that one generation will not be doomed to repeat the tragic errors of its parents. Suddenly, childhood is *past;* it retreats to a darkly romantic and altogether poignant legend, a "fiction" of surpassing beauty but belonging to a remote time.

As the stylized gothic romance yields to something approaching "realism," the artfully fractured chronology begins to sort itself out, as if we are waking rapidly from a dream, and the present time of September 1802 *is* the authentic present, for both the diarist Lockwood and the inhabitants of Wuthering Heights. Mysteries are gradually dispelled; we have gained a more certain footing; as Lockwood makes his way to the Heights, he notes that "all that remained of day was a beamless, amber light along the west; but I could see every pebble on the path, and every blade of grass by that splendid moon." The shift from the gothic sensibility has been prepared from the very first, by Brontë's systematically detailed settings, which are rendered in careful prose by the narrators Lockwood and Mrs. Dean—the only characters we might reasonably expect to *see* the Heights, the Grange, and the moors. The romantic lovers consume themselves in feeling; they feel deeply enough but their feeling relates only to themselves, and excludes the rest of the world. But the narrators, and, through them, the reader, are privileged to see. (It is significant that the ghost-lovers of the older generation walk the moors on rainy nights, and that the lovers of the new generation walk by moonlight.)

For all that she has been demeaned as ordinary, unimaginative, and incapable of comprehending a "grand passion" of the operatic scale of Catherine's and Heathcliff's, the novel's central narrator, Ellen Dean, in her solitary fashion, remains unshakably faithful to the actual world in which romance burns itself out: the workaday world of "splendidly reflected" light and heat, and smooth white paving stone, and high-backed chairs, and immense pewter vessels and tankards, and kitchens cheerful with great fires. Never has the physical world been rendered with more precision, and more obvious sympathy, whether it is the primitive outer world of the moors, or the interiors of the houses; that curious and endlessly fascinating oak-paneled bed, with "squares cut out near the top, resembling coach windows"; Miss Catherine Earnshaw's silken costume, when she returns from five weeks at the Grange; the pipes old Joseph smokes, with evident pleasure. "I smelt the rich scent of the heating spices," Mrs. Dean reports, "and admired the shining kitchen utensils, the polished clock, decked in holly, the silver mugs ranged on a tray ready to be filled with mule ale for supper; and, above all, the speckless purity of my particular care—the scoured and well-swept floor. I gave due inward applause to every object. . . ."[13]

It is this fidelity to the observed physical world, and Brontë's own inward applause, that makes the metamorphosis of the dark tale into its opposite so plausible, as well as so ceremonially appropriate. Though the grave is misjudged by certain persons as a place of fulfillment, the world is not after all phantasmal: it is by daylight that love survives. Long misread as a poetic and metaphysical work given a sort of sickly, fevered radiance by way of the "narrowness" of Emily Brontë's imagination, *Wuthering Heights* can be more accurately be seen as a work of mature and astonishing magnitude. The poetic and the "prosaic" are in exquisite harmony; the metaphysical is balanced by the physical. An anomaly, a sport, a freak in its own time, it can be seen by us, in ours, as brilliantly of that time—and contemporaneous with our own.

Charles Dodgson's Golden Hours

In Charles Lutwidge Dodgson, Oxford clergyman and Mathematical Lecturer of Christ Church, we have the phenomenon of the artist "created" by the processes of his own uncanny imagination: the artist involved in a charming masquerade (in which, at the very least, two almost distinct personalities coexist); the artist as suitor, as swain, as chaste gold-hatted lover, a bachelor steadfast in his loyalty to the child-objects of his adoration but invariably—and necessarily—betrayed. ("The love of children is a fleeting thing," Dodgson once observed.) If the inimitable *Alice* books celebrate play within their frames (that is, in Alice's timeless child-present) and read as elegies beyond those frames (when, for instance, Alice runs home to tea and leaves us in the company of her older sister at *Wonderland's* conclusion); if *The Hunting of the Snark: An Agony in Eight Fits* celebrates loss, madness, violent death, and "soft and sudden vanishing," as well as the comic impotence of "paper, portfolio, pens, /And ink in unfailing supplies," it is nevertheless the case that these works are triumphant affirmations of the will-to-creativity itself, feats of the imagination *sui generis*.

One wonders, is "Lewis Carroll" the explicit creation or persona of Charles Dodgson; or is "Lewis Carroll," like the famous works of fiction published under his name, an archetypal expression of the involuntary processes of art?—the unerring selection of memorable images, the instinctive storytelling strategies, the diabolical mastery of what the reader might *will* for art, in compensation for the irresolutions of life. Dodgson is the perennial enigma, Carroll his creation, in the way in which dreams are "our" creations. It was even claimed by observers that the two sides of Dodgson/Carroll's face did not match.

Inventing the first *Alice* book, constructing that most relentlessly artful of poems, the *Snark*, seem to have been primarily a matter of allowing the unconscious to speak. Judging from Dodgson's testimony concerning the events of July 4, 1862, the "invention" of Alice as a fiction had everything to do, and most directly, with the presence of the child Alice Liddell on a rowing expedition from Folly Bridge to Godstow. "Lewis Carroll" is born as Dodgson begins a story plopping his heroine "straight down a rabbit-hole, without the least idea what was to happen afterwards." (The Reverend Robinson Duckworth, a fellow of Trinity, later recalled the remarkable circumstances of that expedition: "The story was actually composed and spoken *over my shoulder* for the benefit of Alice Liddell. I remember turning round and saying, 'Dodgson, is this an extemporary romance of yours?' And he replied, 'Yes, I'm inventing as we go along.' I remember how, when we had conducted the three children back to the Deanery, Alice said, as she bade us good-night, 'Oh, Mr. Dodgson, I wish you would write out Alice's Adventures for me!' . . .")[1] As for the composition of the *Snark,* has any work, "nonsensical" or otherwise, sprung from a less likely source?

> I was walking on a hillside, alone, one bright summer day, when suddenly there came into my head one line of verse—one solitary line—"For the Snark *was* a Boojum, you see." I knew not what it

meant, then: I know not what it means, now; but I wrote it down: and, some time afterwards, the rest of the stanza occurred to me, that being its last line: and so by degrees, at odd moments during the next year or two, the rest of the poem pieced itself together, that being its last stanza.[2]

(Dodgson is forty-two years old on this July afternoon in 1874, by now "Lewis Carroll," the famous author of the *Alice* books.) There is no reason to believe Dodgson excessively modest, or disingenuous, in his pronounced use of the passive voice (". . . the poem *pieced itself* together"). The animistic nature of Alice's Underground and Looking-Glass worlds as well as the fluidity with which creatures metamorphose into one another, or into "lifeless" objects, must have been a metaphoric expression of Dodgson's own spontaneity. For this is the real thing, the primitive and unmistakable flow of the unconscious as it exerts pressure upon consciousness, demanding translation into language or images (Dodgson also drew with an inspired amateur's skill). It is simply not the case, as Humpty Dumpty so brashly states, that one can make words mean what he chooses, that one can be "master" of language—or of anything. The dream eventually dissolves. The Bellman tingles his pitiless bell.

The *Alice* books and the *Snark* constitute unique literary experiments in their employment of the elements—the trappings, one might say—of a didactic and resolutely pious Victorian sensibility in the service of an anarchic imagination. The mythos of doubleness of that fascinating era (Dr. Jekyll and Mr. Hyde, Dorian Gray and his "miraculous" portrait come immediately to mind, as well as Dodgson/Carroll) allows a fictional underground or looking-glass world in which formal balance is thwarted repeatedly,[3] logic and common sense are always suspended, and the disorienting fact is not that most people are mad but that they appear to be quite content in that condition. (The question *Why?* is answered curtly by *Why not?*—the supreme epigram of the dream-world, as it is very likely the supreme epigram of "our" world.) Riddles without answers are more pointedly riddles than riddles *with* answers; dream-figures are uncivil and "rude" (Alice is always recoiling from rudeness) because they speak as they think, in a single gesture. A game like the famous Caucus Race violates our expectations of what a "game" should be *("Everybody* has won, and all must have prizes"—"But who is to give the prizes?"), however humanitarian and even Christian it seems. The significance of teatime rapidly diminishes if it is *always* teatime, and the dirty cups and saucers are never changed. One may be obliged to run very rapidly in order to keep one's place in the Looking-Glass world, or go backward in order to go forward; whatever solutions or answers are provided, one can be assured that they will trickle through the head "like water through a sieve." And so on, and so forth. Dodgson's images and metaphors are always brilliant. Above all we are haunted by the sense of a coterminous but invisible "real" world to which the *Alice* books and the *Snark*—including their illustrations by Tenniel, Holiday, and contemporary artists like Barry Moser—provide a sort of hallucinatory mirror.

Dodgson's moods are playful, maddening, elegiac. It has been remarked that Alice is solitary, despite the carnival busyness of her narratives, and it is certainly the case that the poor child has every reason to be thoughtful. For *eating* and *being eaten* are major preoccupations of the books, as many a commentator has noted. DRINK ME: to shut up like a telescope, to a height of ten inches—which arouses some natural anxiety in Alice for, after all, it might end "in my going out altogether, like a candle. I wonder what I should be like then?" EAT ME: to open out like the largest telescope that ever was, neck elongated as a swan's: whereupon one is mistaken for the serpent-predator one actually is. The Walrus and the Carpenter devour their trusting oyster charges, and Looking-Glass insects like the Bread-and-butterfly have a hard time of it in the Darwinian struggle for survival. This particular reader, as a very young child, found most terrifying the conclusion of the Looking-Glass feast when all that has been systematically denied becomes possible—becomes manifest. Madness is given a spin of logic. Candles rise to the ceiling, bottles take on plates and forks for limbs, the nightmare is nearly uncontrollable when Alice discovers that the guests are about to be eaten by their "food":

At this moment she heard a hoarse laugh at her side, and turned to see what was the matter with the White Queen, but, instead of the Queen, there was the leg of mutton sitting in a chair. "Here I am!" cried a voice from the soup tureen, and Alice turned again, just in time to see the Queen's broad, good-natured face grinning at her for a moment over the edge of the tureen, before she disappeared into the soup. There was not a moment to be lost. Already several of the guests were lying down in the dishes, and the soup ladle was walking up the table toward Alice's chair, and beckoning to her impatiently to get out of its way.

Since these are children's tales, however, the final triumph is Alice's: she defeats the Looking-Glass world (and cannibalism), and the rapacious adults of Wonderland (who are "nothing but a pack of cards") simply by waking up. She wakes from her dreams; she saves herself, or is saved, by returning to the "sane" world that encloses and defines the nightmare. *Eating* and *being eaten* may be facts of life in the daytime world, but these facts will be withheld from a child's consciousness, just as the unchecked passion of certain female figures—the Red Queen, the Duchess—submits to a tactful Victorian repression. In Wonderland's courtroom, rules are invented on the spot and sentences are pronounced first, verdicts afterwards: if this is a "fact" of Victorian society it need not impress itself upon girls like Alice. (As Dodgson frankly said, concerning *Alice's* probable audience: "My own idea is, that it isn't a book *poor* children would much care for.") Alice's vertiginous changes of size and her frequently expressed fears of becoming extinguished will be postponed altogether, for they are scarcely concerns childhood can accommodate. In *Wonderland* Alice is imagined in the sketchy concluding frame as a "grown woman" who "would keep, through all her riper years, the simple and loving heart of her childhood"—a somewhat perfunctory gesture on Dodgson's part, since the older, *riper* Alice is hardly the Alice he wants to honor and immortalize. In *Looking-Glass's* similarly conventional frame the child Alice (now more conspicuously a "child" than she was in her turbulent dream) plays with her kitten, and quizzes it on the knotty philosophical issue of who might be dreaming whom, but the danger of the Red King's awakening and Alice's subsequent extinction is clearly past.

Since she never dissolves into helpless tears and is never paralyzed by terror we know that Alice is not a real child but a fantasy-child, a heroine: as Robert Graves has said, "the prime heroine of our nation." Her resourcefulness, her unfailing curiosity, her rationalist spirit, and her instinctive sense of fair play and justice make her "ours" in a way that is immensely satisfying to both children and adults, so that Dodgson's early title for *Wonderland—Alice's Golden Hours*—is not altogether inappropriate.

By contrast, *The Hunting of the Snark: An Agony in Eight Fits* has a distinctive—indeed, an obsessive—voice, but no consciousness at its center. Whoever is telling the tale quietly informs us of the disastrous results of the hunt, just as he, or it, informed Dodgson on his afternoon stroll in 1874, of a nonsensical conclusion—"For the Snark *was* a boojum, you see"—that doesn't altogether accommodate the horrific episodes that have transpired. Henry Holiday's extraordinary illustrations for the *Snark,* so literal and meticulous in detail, so serenely mad overall, are the perfect expression of the Snark's voice: distant, detached, occasionally mock "intimate," knowing, bemused: a voice in a sense *outside the frame,* seeing past and future with equal effortlessness, and acknowledging, unlike the narrative voice of the Alice books, not the slightest sympathy with his subject. Alice is always protected by Lewis Carroll's love; the adult men of the Snark expedition—and that Beaver said to be of dubious gender[4]—are on their own. The Snark is one of those chimerical figures upon which we are invited to project any number of meanings, just as the doomed crew of Ahab's *Pequod* see many things in Moby Dick, including a prodigious quantity of blubber. (Hence theories have been advanced identifying the Snark hunt with the quest for material wealth, social advancement, business success in general; and the philosopher Ferdinand Canning Scott Schiller ingeniously argued, in a parody issue of *Mind* of 1901,[5] that Dodgson was satirizing the Hegelian philosopher's circumlocutory search for the Absolute.) Despite such quasi-rational explanations the *Snark* as a reading or listening experience is unmistakable in its pessimism and cruelty—the obverse of Carroll/ Dodgson's sentimentality, perhaps. Since there is no innocent center of consciousness in the midst of the obsessed Snark hunters there is no one fated to survive, save perhaps the Bellman, or the maddening sound of his bell; the final lines belong to the bodiless narrator, and to no one within the poem. The mockery of the conclusion is underscored by its very mildness of expression.

The Hunting of the Snark pitilessly addresses itself to those adults for whom "golden afternoons" are but an intrusive memory, for these are the men—surely Dodgson's satire *is* aimed against masculinity?— who have given up their souls in the Snark-hunt. (Seeking it with thimbles, care, forks, hope; threatening its life with a "railway-share"; charming it—evidently to no avail—with "smiles and soap.") Children are innocent and immortal, adults are fallen and mortal, and one may as well make jokes at their expense, as Balzac and Dickens did as well. (Though it seems clear that the ballad is innocently nonsensical in its opening stanzas, all play and improvised drollery, until, perhaps, the revelation concerning the Butcher, which is reminiscent of Alice's faux pas involving her cat Dinah, in the opening pages of *Wonderland*.)

If the *Snark* seems to gain power as it proceeds, this is a consequence of the outrageous distance between the ballad's fatuous jangling rimes and the grim story it actually tells us. In the seventh fit the Banker goes mad, or suffers a stroke, or undergoes a witty sort of reversal (like a photographic negative—black where white should be) in these childlike intonations:

> He was black in the face, and they scarcely could trace
>   The least likeness to what he had been:
> While so great was his fright that his waistcoat turned white—
>   A wonderful thing to be seen!

> To the horror of all who were present that day,
>   He uprose in full evening dress,
> And with senseless grimaces endeavoured to say
>   What his tongue could no longer express.

(One notes in passing the eerie detachment of "a wonderful thing *to be seen*.")

Yet the hunt for the Snark increases in frenzied zeal, and in the final fit, the eighth, an already nameless hunter, the Baker (variously called "Thingumbob," "Fritter my wig," "What-was-his-name") vanishes before his comrades' eyes:

> They gazed in delight, while the Butcher exclaimed
> "He was always a desperate wag!"
> They beheld him—their Baker—their hero unnamed—
> On top of a neighbouring crag,
>
> Erect and sublime, for one moment of time.
> In the next, that wild figure they saw
> (As if stung by a spasm) plunge into a chasm,
> While they waited and listened in awe.

The Baker's exclamation fades to absolute silence. And not a button, or feather, or mark remains of him afterward:

> In the midst of the word he was trying to say,
> In the midst of his laughter and glee,
> He had softly and suddenly vanished away—
> For the Snark *was* a Boojum, you see.

It has not been a piece of irrelevant information that the Snark always looks grave at a pun.

John Updike's American Comedies

> . . . I must go to Nature disarmed of perspective and
> stretch myself like a large transparent canvas upon her in
> the hope that, my submission being perfect, the imprint
> of a beautiful and useful truth would be taken.
>
> —*The Centaur*

John Updike's genius is best excited by the lyric possibilities of tragic
events that, failing to justify themselves as tragedy, turn unaccount-
ably into comedies. Perhaps it is out of a general sense of doom, of
American expansion and decay, of American subreligions that spring
up so effortlessly everywhere, that Updike works, or perhaps it is
something more personal, which his extraordinarily professional art
can disguise: the constant transformation of what would be "suffering" into works of art that are direct appeals to the *her* of the above
quotation, not for salvation as such, but for the possibly higher
experience of being "transparent," that is, an artist. There has been
from the first, in his fiction, an omniscience that works against the
serious development of tragic experiences; what might be tragedy
can be reexamined, reassessed, and dramatized as finally comic, with
overtones of despair. Contending for one's soul with Nature is, of

course, the Calvinist God Whose judgments may be harsh but do not justify the term *tragic*.

Like Flannery O'Connor, who also studied art before she concentrated upon prose fiction, Updike pays homage to the visual artist's "submission" to the physical stimuli of his world far more than most writers. He transcribes the world for us, and at the same time transcribes the experience of doing so, from the inside. His world, like O'Connor's, is "incarnational"—vividly, lovingly, at times meanly recorded—perhaps because, in Updike, such a synthesis of fidelity and inventiveness allows an escape of sorts from the tyrannical, unimaginative cosmology of Calvinism. O'Connor was affirming her faith through allegorical art: Updike usually affirms it in words, but the act of writing itself, the free lovely spontaneous play of the imagination, *is* salvation of a kind. Does the artist require anything further? Updike's prose style resembles Nabokov's in certain respects and yet in Updike the activity of art is never for Nabokovian purposes—never to deceive, to conceal, to mock, to reduce Nature to an egoistic and mechanical arrangement of words. On the contrary, Updike seems at times too generous, too revealing. His energies are American in their prolific and reverential honoring of a multitude of objects, as Nature is scaled down, compressed, at times hardly more than a series of forms of The Female.

The title story of *Museums and Women* makes the point explicitly that "museums" and "women" are both mysterious structures which, once entered, once explored, inevitably lose their mystery. In the beginning the museum is explored with the boy's mother, under her curiously wordless guidance: "Who she was was a mystery so deep it never formed into a question." Some years later the boy sights the girl who will become his wife on the steps of a museum; she is a fine arts student, a "pale creature," an "innocent sad blankness" where he felt he must stamp his name. In the Guggenheim Museum the narrator, now married, experiences an indefinable enchantment in the presence of another woman, a slight acquaintance whom he never comes to know more intimately; and still later, he walks in the Frick Collection with a woman whom he loves, or believes he loves, very much. Their love is "perfect"—or so it seems. But the women, he realizes, are nameless. As museums are nameless. One turns a corner in the Louvre and confronts the head of a sphinx whose body is displayed in Boston. "So, too, the women were broken arcs of one curve."

Significantly, the lovers part in a museum. Their love, powerful as it seemed, could not endure. And the narrator concludes, sadly:

> I looked back, and it came to me that nothing about museums is as splendid as their entrances—the sudden vault, the shapely cornices, the motionless uniformed guard like a wittily disguised archangel. . . . And it appeared to me that now I was condemned, in my search for the radiance that had faded behind me, to enter more and more museums, and to be a little less exalted by each new entrance, and a little more quickly disenchanted by the familiar contents beyond.[1]

Yet women are, as Peter Caldwell, adolescent hero of *The Centaur,* says, "high religious walls" that attract the artist, as they attract the lover, again and again.

Flannery O'Connor's interest was in love of a distinctly spiritual nature, but Updike speaks with Alexander Blok, surely, in saying, "We love the flesh: its taste, its tones/Its charnel odor, breathed through Death's jaws . . ."[2] Because O'Connor's Catholic faith was unshakable, she could invent for her allegorical people ghastly physical-historical fates, assuming that their souls, encompassing but not limited to their egos, were unkillable. Updike's faith is possibly unshakable as well, which, judging from observations scattered throughout his writing, in a way alarms and amuses him, but his sympathies are usually with those who doubt, who have given up hope of salvation as such, wanting instead to be transparent, artists of their own lives. The "beautiful and useful truth" that Peter Caldwell prayed for has little to do with religious convictions, but everything to do with the patient, reverential transcribing of Man comically descended into the flesh: into Nature. Once in the flesh, once individualized, Man can then attempt some form of rebellion against "fate"—enjoying the very absurdity of his position.

The hero of *Couples,* Piet Hanema, is a man of artistic imagination, somehow trapped by his work, his marriage, the unholy and entertaining town of Tarbox, and he is, despite his despair and his promiscuity, a religious man. Foxy, Piet's mistress, tells him that "his callousness, his promiscuity, had this advantage for her; with him she could be as whorish as she wanted, that unlike most men he really didn't judge." Piet answers that it is his Calvinism: "Only God judged." But more than this, Piet believes that God has already judged: it is all over, history, melodrama, comic arrangements and rearrangements of adulterous couples, the Day of Judgment is—as Kafka has said—a perpetual event, the court always in session and the judgments known ahead of time because everything is predestined.. Updike understands women well in allowing Foxy to compliment her lover on character traits that, ironically, activate less than admirable traits in her, but she speaks more generally for the sly truth that must gradually but inevitably dawn upon the Puritan Calvinist of any intellectual capacity: one can do exactly as one wishes, since salvation or damnation are accomplished facts, impersonal, boring, finally irrelevant. A sense of determinism, whether religious or economic or biological, has personal advantages never dreamt of by those who believe in free will. When Updike explores the non-Protestant possibilities of the imagination, when he sends out his soul, let us say, in the guise of an atheistic Jew, we have the fantastically funny and despairing Bech who, in being elected to a society of arts and letters to which Updike was himself elected in real life, and precociously, muses:

> His mother was out there in that audience! . . . But she had died four years ago, in a nursing home in Riverdale. As the applause washed in, Bech saw that the old lady . . . was not his mother but somebody else's. . . . The light in his eyes turned to warm water. His applause ebbed away. He sat down. . . . Bech tried to clear his vision by contemplating the backs of the heads. They were blank: blank shabby backs of a cardboard tableau lent substance only by the credulous, by old women and children. His knees trembled, as if after an arduous climb. He had made it, he was here, in Heaven. Now what?[3]

Bech is Updike's projection of an Updike unprotected by women, children, God; though attached to his mother as Updike's characters are often attached to their mothers, he "ascends" to this mock-Heaven only after her death, when it is too late. His adventures must be seen as comic because they are so desperate, so horrible. In this way Updike explores wittily the very real possibilities of a shallow imaginative life "free" of Calvinistic gloom, though it must be said, in my opinion at least, that he does not convince us of Bech's "Jewishness"—Bech is a man without a soul. In the brief reverie "Solitaire," in *Museums and Women,* a husband contemplates leaving his wife for his mistress, but contemplates it only with one part of his mind—the esthetic—since he knows very well that his identity would be lost outside the confining and nourishing circle of wife and children: in fact, he married young, had several children almost at once, in order to assure his being trapped. Bech escaped the trap, but at great cost to his soul.

By isolating those lines from *The Centaur* in which Peter-as-Prometheus speaks so eloquently about submitting himself to Nature, I am deliberately giving more weight to the pagan-classical-artistic-"immoral" side of Updike's imagination than to the Calvinistic, though in fact the two are balanced. *The Centaur,* being a relatively early and emotionally autobiographical work, is valuable in its obvious statement of the dichotomy in the author's imagination between the "pagan" and the "Christian." Critics may well disagree about the merit of the uses to which Updike put his childhood interest in "old Greek folk stories told anew," and surely the example of Joyce's *Ulysses* was always in his mind; but, unlike Joyce, he did not evoke the classical in order to give structure to quantity[4] or to comment ironically upon it, but to provide for himself, for Peter, for George Caldwell, another spiritual dimension in which they might be heroic without fear of being heretical. Significantly, the "pagan" world is really a feminine world; Updike alludes to the whimsical and tyrannical figure of Zeus, but it is Venus Aphrodite who speaks to Chiron at such length in Chapter 1 and even offers to embrace him, though he is part-beast, and Venus Aphrodite in the form of Vera

Hummel, the girls' gym teacher, with whom the young, impression-able Peter Caldwell imagines himself "sharing a house" in a conclud-ing chapter. Venus, not Zeus, presides over the pagan world. Unlike the woman who awaits Peter and his father back on the farm, in that fertile but uncultivated land that is more a burden than a place of retreat, Vera Hummel is all warmth, simplicity, radiance, nourish-ment. *She,* of course, is promiscuous; Cassie Caldwell is someone's faithful wife, herself trapped, complaining and bitter and yet, ulti-mately, fairly satisfied with her lot. Vera is the promise; Cassie the reality. Vera forever beckons, but is not known; Cassie is known. Though Peter and his father return to the farm, and will always return (as the narrator of *Of the Farm* returns—to betray his wife with his mother!),[5] it is Venus Aphrodite who has the power of altering lives without exactly touching them. Here is the adolescent Peter:

> The next two hours were unlike any previous in my life. I shared a
> house with a woman, a woman tall in time, so tall I could not
> estimate her height in years, which at the least was twice mine. A
> woman of overarching fame; legends concerning her lovelife
> circulated like dirty coins in the student underworld. A woman
> fully grown and extended in terms of property and authority; her
> presence branched into every corner of the house. . . . Intimations
> of Vera Hummel moved toward me from every corner of her
> house, every shadow. . . .[6]

Always outside the masculine consciousness, this archetypal creature when embodied, however briefly, in flesh, has the power to awaken, however briefly, the "religious" experience common to the entering of both museums and women; she is life itself, the very force of life, playful, promiscuous as Nature, ultimately uncaring as the ancient Magna Mater was so viciously uncaring of the beautiful adolescent youths she loved, and devoured. Contemplating the naked green lady of the Alton Museum, a fountain-statue, the child Peter is at first troubled by the mechanical logistics of the statue that forbid its ever quenching its thirst; but, artist as he is, manipulator of reality as he will be, he tells himself that at night the statue manages to drink from its own fountain. "The coming of night" released the necessary magic. Because the Venus-figure is experienced as archetypal rather than personal, she is never connected with any specific woman, but may be projected into nearly anyone. She is simple, vital, enchanting, and yet—curiously—she is no threat. Men remain married or, at the most, remarry women with children (like Peggy of *Of the Farm;* like Foxy of *Couples,* one baby alive, one baby aborted, but a mother nevertheless), and as everyone knows Venus is sterile. She has never entered history. Piet Hanema perhaps speaks for Updike in diagnosing his eventual dissatisfaction with one of his mistresses, Georgene, because she made adultery too easy, too delightful, for his "warped nature." And so in *The Centaur* Venus/Vera attracts her opposite, the Reverend March, he whose faith is so unshakable, intact, and infrangible as metal, and "like metal dead." Economically and concisely developed, the Reverend March is a type that appears occasionally in Updike ("The Deacon" is an older, wearier version), and whose function in *The Centaur* is to angrily resist the desperate George Caldwell's desire to speak of theological matters at a basketball game, but, more important, to be the man whose faith is dead and metallic and yet rather wonderful—

> Though he can go and pick it up and test its weight whenever he wishes, it has no arms with which to reach and restrain him. He mocks it.

—and whose faith allows him a psychological insight that, in Updike-as-Peter, would be annihilating, when he muses upon the fact that a woman's beauty depends only upon the man who perceives her: her value is not present to herself, but given to her. "Having been forced to perceive this," the Reverend March is therefore "slow to buy."

Because the Feminine Archetype is always projected outward, and the knowledge of this projection ("valuing"—"pricing," in the Reverend March's crude terminology) cannot be accepted except at the risk of emotional impotence, it is unconsciously denied. It is not seen to be a natural psychological fact, in which the perceiver-artist values, creates, and honors everything he sees—not only women— and in which he himself re-creates himself *as* an artist; it is, instead, a despairing "truth," so grotesque it had better not be admitted. So, Updike puts into the mouth of Janice Angstrom of *Rabbit Redux* words no woman would say, being in one sense obvious and in another sense completely incorrect: "I'm just a cunt. There are millions of us now." And Bech's horrific vision in "Bech Panics" is the stuff of which religious conversions are made, so intense and incredulous is his experience of the falsity of an old faith:

> He looked around the ring of munching females and saw their bodies as a Martian or a mollusc might see them, as pulpy stalks of bundled nerves oddly pinched to a bud of concentration in the head, a hairy bone knob holding some pounds of jelly in which a trillion circuits, mostly dead, kept records, coded motor operations, and generated an excess of electricity that pressed into the hairless side of the head and leaked through the orifices, in the form of pained, hopeful noises and a simian dance of wrinkles. Impossible mirages! A blot on nothingness. And to think that all the efforts of his life—his preening, his lovemaking, his typing— boiled down to the attempt to displace a few sparks . . . within some random other scoops of jelly. . . .[8]

Bech gives voice to suspicions Updike may play with, but cannot take seriously; he knows we are not free, and so Bech's lazy "freedom" is mere fiction, the maniacal cleverness of an intellectual consciousness unhampered by restraint, by the necessary admission of its subordinate position in the universe. And yet—if Bech *were* correct—one would be free of the tyrannical father as well, and free of the need to perform, ceaselessly, the erotic activity that defies him: writing. For Bech, of course, is a writer who cannot write. Updike may write about him but Bech requires a week to compose a three-page introduction to the book. Free, yes, undamned and unhaunted—but whoever wanted such freedom?

Most of the time, however, the projection is not recognized as such: it is experienced in a religious manner, the woman is "adored," she is associated with Nature, is either the Mother herself or a form of the mother—as, significantly, Foxy Whitman is loved when she is pregnant and because she is pregnant; once delivered of her child, her "flat" being somehow disappoints and bewilders her lover, and is in any case the promise of timelessness within the oppressive context of time. Burdened with the difficult responsibility of making men immortal, the woman-as-adorned either tires of the whole thing (as Joan Maple has grown tired in *Museums and Women*) or shares with her adorer a baffled metaphysical rage: *Why* isn't love permanent?

In asking of love that it be permanent, Updike's characters assert their profoundly Christian and historically oriented religious temperament, for not many religions have really promised an "immortality" of the ego, or even the Theistic mechanism to assure this permanence. In Updike, Eros is equated with Life itself, but it is usually concentrated, and very intensely indeed, in terms of specific women's bodies. Hence Bech's terror, his breakdown, hence the fact "monstrous and lovely" Peter discovers in kissing his girl, Penny, that at the center of the world is an absence: "Where her legs meet there is nothing." Because he is an adolescent and will be an artist, Peter still values this "nothing" and equates it with "innocence." *He* experiences his own artistry, through this equation, as Chiron/George Caldwell experiences his own divinity by simply accepting, as an ordinary human being, the fact of mortality. *The Centaur* is the most psychologically satisfying of Updike's numerous books—it may or may not be his "best" book—because it has expressed its author's considerable idealism in the guise of adolescent love, for Woman and for Father, an idealism Updike may not trust in adult terms.

(Or perhaps the world has changed, has become more "adult" and secular and unworthy of redemption—the dismal Tarbox of *Museums and Women* is far less attractive than the same Tarbox of *Couples,* though that was degenerate enough. An earlier novel, *Rabbit Run,* explored quite remorselessly the consequences of a reduced, secularized, "unimagined" world, Updike's conception of Updike-without-talent, Updike trapped in quantity. But the consciousness of a Rabbit Angstrom is so foreign to Updike's own that it seems at times more a point of view, a voicing, of that part of the mind unfertilized by the imagination, than a coherent personality. Rabbit is both a poet and a very stupid young man. A decade later, as Rabbit led back, penned, now finally trapped, he has become an uneasy constellation of opinions, insights, descriptive passages, and various lusts, a character at the center of *Rabbit Redux* called "Harry"; he ends his adventure in a motel room with his own wife, Janice, Venus-led-back; he is exhausted, impotent, but agreeable: *O.K.* The *Yes* of *Ulysses* is the weary *O.K.* of a man imagined as typically "American."[9])

The world itself has not changed, though history—both personal and collective—has certainly changed. *Couples* dramatizes in infinite, comically attentive detail the melodramatic adventures of "typical" Americans in a "typical" though sophisticated town in New England: love vies with the stockmarket in reducing everyone to ruins. Much has been said, some of it by the author himself, of the novel's religious and allegorical structure, which is so beautifully folded in with the flow of life, the workings-out of numerous fates, as to be invisible except in concluding scenes: the Congregational Church is struck by "God's own lightning," its weathercock is removed, Piet discovers in the ruins a pamphlet containing an eighteenth-century sermon that speaks of the "indispensable duty" of all nations to know that "the LORD he is God." Piet is not much of a hero, and does not choose to be heroic. He has, after all, helped arrange for the abortion of a baby both he and his mistress really wanted; but he is one of the few characters in Updike's recent fiction who can somehow synthesize the knowledge of human "valuing" with a religious faith that sustains it while reducing it to scale.

Piet does not require that love be permanent—or even "love." If he is an artist it is at compromises he is best; failing to be an architect, he winds up as a construction inspector for military barracks; failing to keep his wife from divorcing him, he moves on to the next stage, the next compromise. He has not much choice except to compromise his ideal love (Foxy pregnant) with his real love (Foxy the individual). After the desperate violence of his love ebbs he is able to see the woman clearly, not perfect, not even very charming, at times embarrassingly "tough," "whorish," as if performing for him, her waist thickened by childbirth, her luminous being somehow coarsened into the flesh of historical experience. Yet Piet says, without lying, that she is beautiful anyway; he adores her anyway; he marries her and they move to another town where "gradually, among people like themselves, they have been accepted as another couple." The practical wisdom of the novel's concluding sentence may be interpreted as cynicism, or as a necessary and therefore rather comic working out of events that made their claim for tragic grandeur, but fell short.

In this way Piet accepts his own mortality, a movement into adulthood, middle age, in which the adolescent yearnings for an inexpressible transcendence in fleshly terms is put aside. In a powerful paragraph at the end of chapter 3 ("Thin Ice"), Piet has already come to terms with his own death by recognizing that "the future is in the sky. . . . Everything already exists" and this knowledge has the effect of undoing some of the magic of Foxy: "Henceforth he would love her less." The "love" he had experienced for Foxy was a form of delirium in which his terror of death was temporarily obliterated in the body of Venus—but only temporarily, for his real allegiance is to doom, to a future already in existence, a God Who manipulates men according to His inscrutable design.[10]

At the same time Piet articulates what is sometimes kept beneath the level of consciousness in Updike: that the infatuation with surfaces, the artist's-eye aspect of his imagination, is somehow less basic to him than a deeper and more impersonal tendency toward unity, toward the general. After Angela has asked Piet to move out of their home he finds himself with a great deal of time, little to do, very much alone; and out of his loneliness the discovery that

> the world was more Platonic than he suspected. He found he missed friends less than friendship; what he felt, remembering Foxy, was a nostalgia for adultery itself—its adventure, the acrobatics its deceptions demand, the tension of its hidden strings, the new landscapes it makes us master.[11]

By a subtle—but not too subtle—shifting from the relatively restricted third person of "he" to the communal "us" Updike invites his readers to admit, in league with his doomed character, that the particular objects of any kind of infatuation, however idealized, are mere stimuli that activate the inborn responses of "love"; Venus Aphrodite is a figure that somehow unites and in that way attempts to explain a bewildering multiplicity of love-urges, but cannot exist "in herself" and cannot be more permanent than the brain-structure in which these love-urges exist. And yet does this really matter? Lying with Foxy in his squalid rented room Piet makes comic moaning noises, at first disgusting Foxy and then drawing her into imitating him; and Updike comments, again with an ironically confident nineteenth-century omniscience: *We are all exiles who need to bathe in the irrational.*

In a poem, "South of the Alps," the speaker is being driven to Lake Como by a beautiful Italian woman; is seated in the back of the car, terrified at the woman's careless speed while "her chatting lover occupied the death seat." The elements of an essential romance are present: the woman is seen as an "ikon," her beauty is "deep in hock to time" and reckless with itself and the men around it, slavish, adoring, hopeless. The poet sees himself as a "cowardly word-hoarder."

> Of course I adored her, though my fate
> was a midge on her wrist she could twitch away;
> the Old Testament said truly: fear
> is love and love is rigid-making fear.

Unknown in any personal, fleshly sense, unentered, unexplored, Signorina Angeli, an "angel" as finally remote and rejecting as Piet's wife Angela, alarms the poet and has the final line of the poem: "Tell me, why doesn't anything last?" And here it is Venus speaking from the disappointed idealism of the male, promised permanence and yet continually denied it.

"South of the Alps" shows us, in beautifully compressed language, the bewildering locked-in fates of of the adorer and the adored: the masculine consciousness that, having failed to integrate the "Feminine" with its own masculinity, seeing it as essentially pagan and heretical, must continually project it outward; the feminine consciousness that, having taken on the masculine, Faustian quest for permanence, must be forever loved, a beloved, an ikon with nostrils "nice as a skull's." Male and female here unite only through a declaration of their common predicament. A writer who shares Updike's extreme interest in the visual world as well as his obsession with language is Joseph Conrad who, significantly, could imagine the ideal and the real only as hopelessly separate: when the "ideal" is given historical freedom to experience itself in flesh, in action, we have the tragicomedy of *Nostromo,* we have the Feminine Archetype, Mrs. Gould, at the very center of a storm of mirages, each an "ideal," each a masculine fantasy. But Conrad—ironic and witty as he may be—is finally without Updike's redeeming sense of humor. Art itself is not redemptive; but the sudden shifting of point of view that allows for a restoration of sanity is often redemptive. There is an Updike who is forever being driven along dangerous narrow roads by a beautiful woman with an intriguing, because mysterious, past, himself a hoarder of words, hoping only to experience transparency in the face of such wonder; there is another Updike in the guise of Reverend March, knowing his bitter metallic Calvinistic faith so unkillable that he may mock it, betray it, take every possible risk of damnation—because he is already saved, or already damned anyway. And out of this curious duality comes the paradoxical freedom of the true artist: having conquered both his temptation by vice and his temptation by virtue, he may live as ordinarily as anyone else.

The present action of *The Centaur* is a long "dreaming-back" as Peter Caldwell, now a young adult, a painter who lives with his black mistress in a loft in New York City, tortures himself with doubts. *Was it for this that my father gave up his life?* In *Of the Farm* it is mentioned that George Robinson's death may have been hastened—but it is more his wife's fault, probably, than his son's; and in "Flight" it is the mother, eerily powerful, who insists upon the brilliant young boy's flight, his escape from that part of Pennsylvania in which she knows herself trapped, partly by the burden of her own aged but undying father. Yet though Peter worries about the role he may have played in exhausting his father, the novel as a whole works to liberate him from guilt and would be, for this reason alone, an unusual work for an American writer; O'Neill's *A Long Day's Journey into Night* is its exact reverse. The point is made explicitly that the father, in giving his life for others, enters a total freedom. He is the "noblest of all the Centaurs" and certainly the noblest of all the characters in Updike's now vast canvas: it is not Peter's right to doubt.

From George Caldwell's experience, then, comes a conviction that permeates Updike's work even when it appears in secularized and diminished settings: that one cannot assume any ultimate truths about other people, that they forever elude the word-nets we devise. Fearing he had cancer of the bowels, Caldwell had been more or less ready to die and (like Piet Hanema after the missile crisis) feels somewhat cheated after learning that his X-rays are clear, having been "spoiled" by the expectation of an end to his troubled life. Yet he accepts it all again. Life consists and will always consist of some version of Caldwell's lot:

> The prospect of having again to maneuver among Zimmerman and Mrs. Herzog and all that overbearing unfathomable Olinger gang made him giddy, sick; how could his father's seed, exploding into an infinitude of possibilities, have been funnelled into this, this paralyzed patch of thankless alien land, these few cryptic faces, those certain four walls of Room 204?[12]

Yet he accepts it. By doing so he is blessed with the release of death. He is freed of his ego, his concern for himself, and is liberated from the tyranny of the Calvinistic vision of life which his son cannot avoid inheriting. Peter, Prometheus and artist, a Daedalus as well who *must* rebel against so holy a fate in order to honor it through his art, can encompass this wisdom only in the speculative recesses of his dreaming mind—he imagines his father as "saved," but he dare not accept such salvation for himself, because in giving his life to others (particularly to the mother who so blackmails him with her "love") he cannot be an artist.

In assembling the short stories and sketches called, simply, *Olinger Stories,* Updike spoke of having said the "final word" in 1964; by having written *The Centaur* and transforming Olinger into

Olympus, he closed the book on his own adolescence—the past is now a fable, receding, completed. But the past is never completed; it is not even *past*. It is a continual present. And so, having in a way immortalized and killed the "George Caldwell" of *The Centaur,* the author takes on, perhaps unconsciously, those traits he found so exasperating in the man as an adolescent: "Daddy, why are you so—superstitious? You make everything mean something it isn't. Why? Why can't you *relax?* It's so exhausting!" And he has taken on as well that remarkably detached, rather elegantly egoless ability to glance without judgment on all sides of a melodramatic event, a basic clownishness, that seems to go largely unnoticed in his writing, but which gives it its energy, its high worth. Caldwell is funny, very funny, not with Bech's overwrought and neurotic wit, but with a fundamentally amiable acceptance of mystery. He reduces theological arguments to their basic emotional core and, correctly, presents it all as a cosmic joke:

> What I could never ram through my thick skull was why the ones that don't have it [the non-Elect] were created in the first place. The only reason I could figure out was that God had to have somebody to fry down in Hell.[13]

Caldwell's life is a torment but the torment is relieved by his sense of humor, and the sense of humility that so often accompanies humor.

The truly religious imagination is often given energy by a sense of the individual's relative smallness (and, perversely, his significance) that has much to do with the underlying spirit of comedy. It is doubtful that such an imagination can be "tragic"—it may even prove itself zestfully capable, like Flannery O'Connor, of a high-handed burlesque cruelty toward her characters that can alarm the liberal imagination because this cruelty—pratfalls, mass murders, and all—must be interpreted as part of a cosmic joke. The pattern is always for compromise, for a reexamination and scaling down of passions, as we see in the course of Saul Bellow's fiction as well: from the intense subjectivity of *Dangling Man* to the wildly comic (but no less serious)

Humboldt's Gift. Comedy can contain any number of tragic plots because it strives for omniscience, and—very simply—the "omniscient" viewpoint is not a human viewpoint. In Updike, when faith in the spiritual world recedes, a surrogate must appear, or be summoned forth; in any case new people will come along, a new generation, powerful in their innocence (as at the conclusion of *Couples* the socially conscious and "radical" younger generation of citizens is taking possession, rather self-righteously, of Tarbox). If faith is time-bound, historical rather than "eternal," it carries within it the germ, the necessity, of its own disintegration. The process in time is always toward disintegration: the physical conquest of any embodiment of the life-giving Venus is a self-destructing act. And yet— "We love the flesh: its taste, its tones . . ."—what to make of this torment except an art that, being totally transparent, submissive, finally achieves its own immortality?

Notes on Failure

To Whom the Mornings stand for Nights,
What must the Midnights—be!
                                        —EMILY DICKINSON

If writing quickens one's sense of life, like falling in love, like being precariously in love, it is not because one has any confidence in achieving *success,* but because one is most painfully and constantly made aware of *mortality:* the persistent question being, Is this the work I fail to complete, is this the "posthumous" work that can only make an appeal to pity. . . ?

The practicing writer, the writer-at-work, the writer immersed in his or her project, is not an entity at all, let alone a person, but a curious mélange of wildly varying states of mind, clustered toward what might be called the darker end of the spectrum: indecision, frustration, pain, dismay, despair, remorse, impatience, outright failure. To be honored in midstream for one's labor would be ideal, but impossible; to be honored after the fact is always too late, for by then another project has been begun, another concatenation of indefinable states. Perhaps one must contend with vaguely warring personalities, in some sort of sequential arrangement?—perhaps

106

premonitions of failure are but the soul's wise economy, in not risking hubris?—it cannot matter, for, in any case, the writer, however battered a veteran, can't have any real faith, any absolute faith, in his stamina (let alone his theoretical "gift") to get him through the ordeal of *creating,* to the plateau of *creation.* One is frequently asked whether the process becomes easier, with the passage of time, and the reply is obvious: *Nothing gets easier with the passage of time, not even the passing of time.*

The artist, perhaps more than most people, inhabits failure, degrees of failure and accommodation and compromise; but the terms of his failure are generally secret. It seems reasonable to believe that failure may be a truth, or at any rate a negotiable fact, while success is a temporary illusion of some intoxicating sort, a bubble soon to be pricked, a flower whose petals will quickly drop. If despair is—as I believe it to be—as absurd a state of the soul as euphoria, who can protest that it feels more substantial, more reliable, less out of scale with the human environment? When it was observed to T. S. Eliot that most critics are failed writers, Eliot replied: "But so are most writers."

Though most of us inhabit degrees of failure or the anticipation of it, very few persons are willing to acknowledge the fact, out of a vague but surely correct sense that it is not altogether American to do so. *Your standards are unreasonably high, you must be exaggerating, you must be of a naturally melancholy and saturnine temperament.* . . . From this pragmatic vantage point "success" itself is but a form of "failure," a compromise between what is desired and what is attained. One must be stoic, one must develop a sense of humor. And, after all, there is the example of William Faulkner, who considered himself a failed poet; Henry James returning to prose fiction after the conspicuous failure of his play-writing career; Ring Lardner writing his impeccable American prose because he despaired of writing sentimental popular songs; Hans Christian Andersen perfecting his fairy tales since hs was clearly a failure in other genres—poetry, play writing, life. One has only to glance at *Chamber Music* to see why James Joyce specialized in prose.

Whoever battles with monsters had better see that it does not turn him into a monster. And if you gaze too long into an abyss—the abyss will gaze back into you. So Nietzsche cryptically warns us: and it is not implausible to surmise that he knew, so far as his own battles, his own monsters, and his own imminent abyss were concerned, much that lay before him: though he could not have guessed its attendant ironies, or the ignoble shallowness of the abyss. Neither does he suggest an alternative.

The specter of failure haunts us less than the specter of failing—the process, the activity, the absorbing delusionary stratagems. The battle lost, in retrospect, is, after all, a battle necessarily lost to time: and, won or lost, it belongs to another person. But the battle in the process of being lost, each gesture, each pulse beat . . . This is the true abyss of dread, the unspeakable predicament. *To Whom the Mornings stand for Nights,/What must the Midnights—be!*

But how graceful, how extraordinary these pitiless lines, written by Emily Dickinson some four years earlier, in 1862:

> The first Day's Night had come—
> And grateful that a thing
> So terrible—had been endured—
> I told my Soul to sing—
>
> She said her Strings were snapt—
> Her bow—to Atoms blown—
> And so to mend her—gave me work
> Until another Morn—
>
> And then—a Day as huge
> As Yesterdays in pairs,
> Unrolled its horror in my face—
> Until it blocked my eyes—
>
> My Brain—begun to laugh—
> I mumbled—like a fool—
> And tho' 'tis Years ago—that Day—
> My Brain keeps giggling—still.

> And Something's odd—within—
> That person that I was—
> And this One—do not feel the same—
> Could it be Madness—this?

Here the poet communicates, in the most succinct and compelling imagery, the phenomenon of the ceaseless process of *creating:* the instruction by what one might call the ego that the Soul "sing," despite the nightmare of "Yesterdays in pairs"—the valiant effort of keeping language, forging language, though the conviction is overwhelming that "the person that I was—/And this One—do not feel the same." (For how, a scant poem later, *can* they be the same?) And again, in the same year:

> The Brain, within its Groove
> Runs evenly—and true—
> But let a Splinter swerve—
> 'Twere easier for You—
>
> To put a Current back—
> When Floods have slit the Hills—
> And scooped a Turnpike for Themselves—
> And trodden out the Mills—

The Flood that is the source of creativity, and the source of self-oblivion: sweeping away, among other things, the very Soul that would sing. And is it possible to forgive Joseph Conrad for saying, in the midst of his slough of despair while writing *Nostromo,* surely one of the prodigious feats of the imagination in our time, that writing is but the "conversion of nervous force" into language?—so profoundly bleak an utterance that it must be true. For, after all, as the busily productive Charles Gould remarks to his wife, a man must apply himself to *some* activity.

Even that self-proclaimed "teacher of athletes," that vehement rejector of "down-hearted doubters . . . /Frivolous, sullen, moping, angry, affected, dishearten'd, atheistical," that Bard of the American roadway who so wears us out with his yawp of barbaric optimism, and his ebullient energy, even the great Whitman himself confesses in "As I Ebb'd with the Ocean of Life," that things are often quite different, quite different indeed. When one is alone, walking at the edge of the ocean, at autumn, "held by this electric self out of the pride of which I utter poems"—

> O baffled, balk'd, bent to the very earth,
> Oppressed with myself that I have dared to open my mouth,
> Aware now that amid all that blab whose echoes recoil upon me
>   I have not once had the least idea who or what I am,
> But that before all my arrogant poems the real Me stands yet
>   untouch'd, untold, altogether unreach'd,
> Withdrawn far, mocking me with self-congratulatory signs and
>   bows,
> With peals of distant ironical laughter at every word I have
>   written,
> Pointing in silence to these songs, and then to the sand beneath.

Interesting to note that these lines were published in the same year, 1860, as such tirelessly exuberant and more "Whitmanesque" poems as "For You O Democracy," "Myself and Mine" ("Myself and mine gymnastic ever,/To stand the cold or heat, to take good aim with a gun, to sail a/boat, to manage horses, to beget superb children"), and "I Hear America Singing." More subdued and more eloquent is the short poem, "A Clear Midnight," of 1881, which allows us to overhear the poet in his solitude, the poet no longer in the blaze of noon on a public platform:

> This is thy hour O Soul, thy free flight into the wordless,
> Away from books, away from art, the day erased, the lesson
>   done,
> Thee fully forth emerging, silent, gazing, pondering the themes
>   thou lovest best,
> Night, sleep, death and the stars.

One feels distinctly honored, to have the privilege of such moments: to venture around behind the tapestry, to see the threads in their untidy knots, the loose ends hanging frayed.

Why certain individuals appear to devote their lives to the phenomenon of interpreting experience in terms of structure, and of language, must remain a mystery. It is not an alternative to life, still less an escape from life, it *is* life: yet overlaid with a peculiar sort of luminosity, as if one were, and were not, fully inhabiting the present tense. Freud's supposition—which must have been his own secret compulsion, his sounding of his own depths—that the artist labors at his art to win fame, power, riches, and the love of women, hardly addresses itself to the fact that, such booty being won, the artist often intensifies his effort: and finds much of life, apart from that effort, unrewarding. Why, then, this instinct to interpret; to transpose flickering and transient thoughts into the relative permanence of language; to give oneself over to decades of obsessive labor, in the service of an elusive "transcendental" ideal, that, in any case, will surely be misunderstood or scarcely valued at all? Assuming that all art is metaphor, or metaphorical, what really *is* the motive for metaphor? Is there a motive? Or, in fact, metaphor? Can one say anything finally, with unqualified confidence, about any work of art—why it strikes a profound, irresistible, and occasionally life-altering response in some individuals, yet means very little to others? In this, the art of reading hardly differs from the art of writing, in that its most intense pleasures and pains must remain private, and cannot be communicated to others. Our secret affinities remain secret even to ourselves. . . . We fall in love with certain works of art, as we fall in love with certain individuals, for no very clear motive.

In 1955, in the final year of his life, as profusely honored as any writer in history, Thomas Mann wryly observed in a letter that he had always admired Hans Christian Andersen's fairy tale, "The Steadfast Tin Soldier." "Fundamentally," says Mann, "it is the symbol of my life." (And what is the "symbol" of Mann's life? Andersen's toy soldier is futilely in love with a pretty dancer, a paper cutout; his fate is to be cruelly, if casually, tossed into the fire by a child, and melted down to the shape "of a small tin heart.") Like most of Andersen's tales the story of the steadfast tin soldier is scarcely a children's story, though couched in the mock-simple language of childhood; and one can see why Thomas Mann felt such kinship with it, for it begins: "There were once five and twenty tin soldiers, all brothers, for they were the offspring of the same old tin spoon. Each man shouldered his gun, kept his eyes well to the front, and wore the smartest red and blue uniform imaginable. . . . All the soldiers were exactly alike with one exception, and he differed from the rest in having only one leg. For he was made last, and there was not quite enough tin left to finish him. However, he stood just as well on his one leg as the others did on two. In fact he was the very one who became famous."

Is the artist secretly in love with failure? one might ask.

Is there something dangerous about "success," something finite and limited and, in a sense, historical: the passing over from *striving,* and *strife,* to *achievement?* One thinks again of Nietzsche, that most profound of psychologists, who tasted the poisonous euphoria of success, however brief, however unsatisfying: beware the danger in happiness! *Now everything I touch turns out to be wonderful. Now I love any fate that comes along. Who would like to be my fate?*

Yet it is perhaps not failure the writer loves, so much as the addictive nature of incompletion and risk. A work of art acquires, and then demands, its own singular "voice"; it insists upon its integrity; as Gide in his *Notebook* observed, the artist needs "a special world of which he alone has the key." That the fear of dying or becoming seriously ill in midstream is very real, cannot be doubted: and if there is an obvious contradiction here (one dreads completion; one dreads the possibility of a "posthumous" and therefore uncompleted work), that contradiction is very likely at the heart of the artistic enterprise. The writer carries himself as he would carry a precarious pyramid of eggs, because he is, in fact, a precarious pyramid of eggs, in danger of falling at any moment, and shattering on the floor in an ignoble mess. And he understands beforehand that no one, not even his most "sympathetic" fellow writers, will acknowledge his brilliant intentions, and see, for themselves, the great work he would surely have completed, had he lived.

An affinity for risk, danger, mystery, a certain derangement of the soul; a craving for distress, the pinching of the nerves, the not-yet-voiced; the predilection for insomnia; an impatience with past selves and past creations that must be hidden from one's admirers—why is the artist drawn to such extremes, why are we drawn along with him? Here, a forthright and passionate voice, from a source many would think unlikely:

> There are few of us who have not sometimes wakened before dawn, either after one of those dreamless nights that make us almost enamoured of death, or one of those nights of horror and misshapen joy, when through the chambers of the brain sweep phantoms more terrible than reality itself, and instinct with that vivid life that lurks in all grotesques, and that lends to Gothic art its enduring vitality. . . . Veil after veil of thin dusky gauze is lifted, and by degrees the forms and colors of things are restored to them, and we watch the dawn remaking the world in its antique pattern. The wan mirrors get back their mimic life. . . . Nothing seems to us changed. Out of the unreal shadows of the night comes back the real life that we had known. We have to resume it where we had left off, and there steals over us a terrible sense of the necessity for the continuance of energy in the same wearisome round of stereotyped habits, or a wild longing, it may be, that our eyelids might open some morning upon a world that had been refashioned anew in the darkness . . . a world in which the past would have little or no place, or survive, at any rate, in no conscious form of obligation and regret. . . . It was the creation of such worlds as these that seemed to Dorian Gray to be the true object . . . of life.

That this unmistakably heartfelt observation should be bracketed, in Wilde's great novel, by chapters of near-numbing cleverness, and moralizing of a Bunyanesque nature, does not detract from its peculiar poignancy: for here, one feels, Wilde is speaking without artifice or posturing; and that Dorian Gray, freed for the moment from his somewhat mechanical role in the allegory Wilde has assembled, to explain himself to himself, has in fact acquired the transparency—the invisibility—of a mask of our own.

Will one fail is a question less apposite, finally, then *can one succeed?*—granted the psychic predicament, the addiction to a worldly skepticism that contrasts (perhaps comically) with the artist's private system of customs, habits, and superstitious routines that constitutes his "working life." (A study should really be done of artists' private systems, that cluster of stratagems, both voluntary and involuntary, that make daily life navigable. Here we would find, I think, a bizarre and ingenious assortment of Great Religions in embryo—a system of checks and balances, rewards, and taboos, fastidious as a work of art. *What is your work schedule,* one writer asks another, never *What are the great themes of your books?*—for the question is, of course, in code, and really implies *Are you perhaps crazier than I?—and will you elaborate?*)

How to attain a destination is always more intriguing (involving, as it does, both ingenuity and labor) than *what* the destination finally is. It has always been the tedious argument of moralists that artists appear to value their art above what is called "morality"; but is not the artist by definition an individual who has grown to care more about the interior dimensions of his art than about its public aspect, simply because—can this be doubted?—he spends all his waking hours, and many of his sleeping hours, in that landscape?

The curious blend of the visionary and the pragmatic that characterizes most novelists is exemplified by Joyce's attitude toward the various styles of *Ulysses,* those remarkable exuberant self-parodying voices: "From my point of view it hardly matters whether the technique is 'veracious' or not; it has served me as a bridge over which to march my eighteen episodes, and, once I have got my troops across, the opposing forces can, for all I care, blow the bridge sky-high." And though critics generally focus upon the ingenious relationship of *Ulysses* to the *Odyssey,* the classical structure was one Joyce chose with a certain degree of arbitrariness, as he might have chosen another—*Peer Gynt,* for instance; or *Faust.* That the writer labors to discover the secret of his work is perhaps the writer's most baffling predicament, about which he cannot easily speak: for he cannot write the fiction without becoming, beforehand, the person who *must* write that fiction: and he cannot be that person, without first subordinating himself to the process, the labor, of creating that fiction. . . . Which is why one becomes addicted to insomnia itself, to a perpetual sense of things about to fail, the pyramid of eggs about to tumble, the house of cards about to be blown away. Deadpan, Stanislaus Joyce noted in his diary, in 1907: "Jim says that . . . when he writes, his mind is as nearly normal as possible."

But my position, as elaborated, is, after all, only the reverse of the tapestry.

Let us reconsider. Isn't there, perhaps, a very literal advantage, now and then, to failure?—a way of turning even the most melancholy of experiences inside out, until they resemble experiences of *value,* of *growth,* of *profound significance?* That Henry James so spectacularly failed as a playwright had at least two consequences: it contributed to a nervous collapse; and it diverted him from a career for which he was unsuited (not because he had a too grandly "literary" and ambitious conception of the theater but because, in fact, his theatrical aspirations were so conventional, so trivial), thereby allowing him the spaciousness of relative failure. The public catastrophe of *Guy Domville* behind him, James wrote in his notebook: "I take up my *own* old pen again—the pen of all my old unforgettable efforts and sacred struggles. To myself—today—I need say no more. Large and full and high the future still opens. It is now indeed that I may do the work of my life. And I will." *What Maisie Knew, The Awkward Age, The Ambassadors, The Wings of the Dove, The Golden Bowl*—the work of James's life. Which success in the London theater would have supplanted, or would have made unnecessary.

Alice James, the younger sister of William and Henry, was born into a family in which, by Henry's admission, "girls seem scarcely to have had a chance." As her brilliant *Diary* acknowledges, Alice made a career of various kinds of failure: the failure to become an adult; the failure to become a "woman" in conventional terms; the failure— which strikes us as magnificently stubborn—to survive. (When Alice discovered that she had cancer of the breast, at the age of forty-three, she wrote rhapsodically in her diary of her great good fortune: for now her long and questionable career of invalidism had its concrete, incontestable, deathly vindication.)

Alice lies on her couch forever. Alice, the "innocent" victim of fainting spells, convulsions, fits of hysteria, mysterious paralyzing pains, and such nineteenth-century female maladies as nervous hyperesthesia, spinal neurosis, cardiac complications, and rheumatic gout. Alice, the focus of a great deal of familial attention; yet the focus of no one's interest. Lying on her couch she does not matter in the public world, in the world of men, of history. She does not count; she *is* nothing. Yet the *Diary,* revealed to her brothers only after her death, exhibits a merciless eye, an unfailing accurate ear, a talent that rivals "Harry's" (that is, Henry's) for its astuteness, and far surpasses his for its satirical and sometimes cruel humor. Alice James's career-invalidism deprives her of everything; yet, paradoxically, of nothing. The triumph of the *Diary* is the triumph of a distinct literary voice, as valuable as the voice of Virginia Woolf's celebrated diaries.

> I think if I get into the habit of writing a bit about what happens, or rather what doesn't happen, I may lose a little of the sense of loneliness and isolation which abides with me. . . . Scribbling my notes and reading [in order to clarify] the density and shape the formless mass within. Life seems inconceivably rich.

Life seems inconceivably rich—the sudden exclamation of the writer, the artist, in defiance of external circumstances.

The invalid remains an invalid. She dies triumphantly young. When a nurse wished to commiserate with her about her predicament, Alice notes in her diary that destiny—any destiny—because it *is* destiny—is fascinating: thus pity is unnecessary. One is born not to suffer but to negotiate with suffering, to choose or invent forms to accommodate it.

Every commentator feels puritanically obliged to pass judgment on Alice. As if the *Diary* were not a document of literary worth; as if it doesn't surpass in literary and historical interest most of the publications of Alice's contemporaries, male or female. This "failure" to realize one's gifts may look like something very different from within. One must remember that, in the James family, "an interesting failure had more value than too-obvious success"—as it does to most observers.

In any case Alice James creates "Alice," a possibly fictitious person, a marvelous unforgettable voice. It is Alice who sinks unprotesting into death; it is Alice who says: "I shall proclaim that anyone who spends her life as an appendage to five cushions and three shawls is justified in committing the sloppiest kind of suicide at a moment's notice."

In Cyril Connolly's elegiac "war-book" *The Unquiet Grave: A Word Cycle by Palinurus,* the shadowy doomed figure of Palinurus broods upon the melancholic but strengthening wisdom of the ages, as a means of "contemplating" (never has the force of that word been more justified), and eventually rejecting, his own suicide. Palinurus, the legendary pilot of Aeneas, becomes for the thirty-nine-year-old Connolly an image of his own ambivalence, which might be called "neurotic" and self-destructive, unless one recalls the specific historical context in which the idiosyncratic "word cycle" was written, between the autumn of 1942 and the autumn of 1943, in London. *The Unquiet Grave* is a journal in perpetual metamorphosis; a lyric assemblage of epigrams, reflections, paradoxes, and descriptive passages; a commonplace book in which the masters of European literature from Horace and Virgil to Goethe, Schopenhauer, Flaubert, and beyond, are employed, as voices in Palinurus's meditation. In "Lemprière," Palinurus suffered a fate that, in abbreviated form, would appear to cry out for retribution, as well as pity:

> Palinurus, a skillful pilot of the ship of Aeneas,
> fell into the sea in his sleep, was three days exposed
> to the tempests and waves of the sea, and at last came
> to the sea shore near Velia, where the cruel inhabitants
> of the place murdered him to obtain his clothes: his
> body was left unburied on the seashore.

Connolly's meditation upon the temptations of death takes the formal structure of an initiation, a descent into hell, a purification, a cure—for "the ghost of Palinurus must be appeased." Approaching forty, Connolly prepares to "heave his carcass of vanity, boredom, guilt and remorse into another decade." His marriage has failed; the France he has loved is cut off from him, as a consequence of the war; it may well be that the world as he has known it will not endure. He considers the rewards of opium-smoking, he broods upon the recent suicides of four friends, he surrenders his lost Eden and accommodates himself to a changed but evidently enduring world. The word cycle ends with an understated defense of the virtues of happiness, by way of a close analysis of Palinurus's complicity in his fate.

> As a myth . . . with a valuable psychological interpretation, Palinurus clearly stands for a certain will-to-failure or repugnance-to-success, a desire to give up at the last moment, an urge toward loneliness, isolation, and obscurity. Palinurus, in spite of his great ability and his conspicuous public position, deserted his post in the moment of victory and opted for the unknown shore.

Connolly rejects his own predilection for failure and self-willed death only by this systematic immersion in "Palinurus's" desire for the unknown shore: *The Unquiet Grave* achieves its success as a unique work by way of its sympathy with failure.

Early failure, "success" in being published of so minimal a nature it might be termed failure, repeated frustrations, may have made James Joyce possible: these factors did not, at any rate, humble him.

Consider the example of his first attempt at a novel, *Stephen Hero,* a fragmented work that reads precisely like a "first novel"—ambitious, youthful, flawed with the energies and naïve insights of youth, altogether conventional in outline and style, but, one would say, "promising." (Though conspicuously less promising than D. H. Lawrence's first novel, *The White Peacock.*) Had Joyce found himself in a position to publish *Stephen Hero,* had his other publishing experiences been less disheartening, he would have used the material that constitutes *A Portrait of the Artist as a Young Man;* and that great novel would not have been written. As things evolved, Joyce retreated, and allowed himself ten years to write a masterpiece: and so he rewrote *Stephen Hero* totally, using the first draft as raw material upon which language makes a gloss. *Stephen Hero* presents characters and ideas, tells a story: *A Portrait of the Artist* is about language, *is* language, a portrait-in-progress of the creator, as he discovers the range and depth of his genius. The "soul in gestation" of Stephen Dedalus gains its individuality and its defiant strength as the novel proceeds; at the novel's conclusion it has even gained a kind of autonomy, wresting from the author a *first-person* voice, supplanting the novel's strategy of narration with Stephen's own journal. Out of unexceptional and perhaps even banal material Joyce created one of the most original works in our language. If the publication of *Dubliners* had been less catastrophic, however, and a clamor had arisen for the first novel by this "promising" young Irishman, one might imagine a version of *Stephen Hero* published the following year: for, if the verse of *Chamber Music* (Joyce's first book) is any measure, Joyce was surely not a competent critic of his own work at this time; and, in any case, as always, he needed money. If *Stephen Hero* had been published, *Portrait* could not have been written; without *Portrait,* its conclusion in particular, it is difficult to imagine the genesis of *Ulysses* . . . So one speculates; so it seems likely, in retrospect. But James Joyce was protected by the unpopularity of his work. He enjoyed, as his brother Stanislaus observed, "that inflexibility firmly rooted in failure."

The possibilities are countless. Can one imagine a D. H. Lawrence whose great novel *The Rainbow* had enjoyed a routine popular fate, instead of arousing the most extraordinary sort of vituperation ("There is no form of viciousness, of suggestiveness, that is not reflected in these pages," said a reviewer for one publication; the novel, said another reviewer, "had no right to exist"); how then could *Women in Love,* fueled by Lawrence's rage and loathing, have been written? And what of the evangelical *Lady Chatterly's Lover,* in its several versions? In an alternative universe there is a

William Faulkner whose poetry (variously, and ineptly, modeled on Swinburne, Eliot, and others) was "successful"; there is a Faulkner whose early, derivative novels gained him a substantial public and commercial success—imitation Hemingway in *Soldiers Pay,* imitation Huxley in *Mosquitoes*—with the consequence that Faulkner's own voice might never have developed. (For when Faulkner needed money—and he always needed money—he wrote as rapidly and as pragmatically as possible.) That his great, idiosyncratic, difficult novels *(The Sound and the Fury, As I Lay Dying, Light in August, Absalom, Absalom!)* held so little commercial promise allowed him the freedom, the spaciousness, one might even say the privacy, to experiment with language as radically as he wished: for it is the "inflexibility" of which Stanislaus Joyce spoke that genius most requires.

But the genius cannot know that he is a genius—not really: he has hopes, he has premonitions, he suffers raging paranoid doubts, but he can have, in the end, only himself for measurement. Success is distant and illusory, failure one's loyal companion, one's stimulus for imagining that the next book will be better, for, otherwise, why write? The impulse can be made to sound theoretical, and even philosophical, but it is, no doubt, as physical as our blood and marrow. *This insatiable desire to write something before I die, this ravaging sense of the shortness and feverishness of life, make me cling . . . to my one anchor*—so Virginia Woolf, in her diary, speaks for us all.

REVIEWS

The Interior Castle

THE ART OF JEAN STAFFORD'S
SHORT FICTION

Certainly the stories are exquisitely wrought, sensitively imagined: like glass flowers, or arabesques, or the "interior castle" of Pansy Vanneman's brain ("Not only the brain as the seat of consciousness, but the physical organ itself which she envisioned, romantically, now as a jewel, now as a flower, now as a light in a glass, now as an envelope of rosy vellum containing other envelopes, one within the other, diminishing infinitely"). Dramatic tension is subdued, in a sense forced underground, so that while narrative conflict between individuals is rare, an extraordinary pressure is built up within the protagonists, who appear trapped inside their own heads, inside their lives (or the social roles their "lives" have become), and despair of striking free. Intelligence and self-consciousness and even a measure of audacity are not quite enough to assure freedom, as the heroines of the late stories "Beatrice Trueblood's Story" and "The End of a Career" discover painfully; even "the liberation" of Polly Bay (in the

123

story with that title) will strike the sympathetic reader as desperate, an adolescent's gesture. The finest of Jean Stafford's stories possess an eerily elegiac tone, though they are never morbid or self-pitying. "In the Zoo" tells a frightful tale, the narrator confesses that "my pain becomes intolerable," but the story concludes with an extravagant outburst of paranoia that manages to be comic as well as distressing; and poor Ramona/Martha Dunn of the early story "The Echo and the Nemesis," trapped within layers of fat, achieves a sort of grotesque triumph over the "normal" and unimaginative Sue, who can only flee in terror the spirited (and insatiable) appetite Ramona represents. ("I am exceptionally ill," Ramona tells her friend, with as much pride as if she were saying, "I am exceptionally talented" or "I am exceptionally attractive.")

This is an art that curves inward toward the meditative, the reminiscent, given life not by bold gestures or strokes but by a patient accumulation of sharply observed impressions: the wealth of a poet's eye, or a painter's. "The Lippia Lawn," for instance, is an exercise in recollection, so graphically presented as to allow the reader to share in the young woman's grasping, groping effort to isolate an image out of her past. The "friendless old bachelor" Mr. Oliphant, while an arresting character in himself, is far less real than the protagonist's thoughts—the "interior castle" of her subjectivity. She half listens to the old man's chatter as "the tenuous memory wove in and out of my thoughts, always tantalizingly just ahead of me. Like the butterfly whose yellow wings are camouflaged to look like sunlight, the flower I could not remember masqueraded as arbutus. . . . Slowly, like a shadow, the past seeped back. A wise scout was reconnoitering for me and at last led me to a place where I never would have looked." In the deceptively tranquil, slow-moving "A Country Love Story" the young wife May eludes her husband Daniel—the tyranny of his almost reasonable madness—by imagining for herself a lover, a lover whose natural place is in an antique sleigh in the front yard of their home. The lover possesses a ghostly plausibility: ". . . there was a delicate pallor on his high, intelligent forehead and there was an invalid's languor in his whole attitude. He wore a white blazer and gray flannels and there was a yellow rosebud in his lapel. Young as he was, he did not, even so, seem to belong to her generation; rather, he seemed to be the reincarnation of someone's uncle as he had been fifty years before." Escaping the oppressive authority of her cerebral husband, May drifts into a sinister, because more seductive and satisfying, predicament; by the story's end she and Daniel have traded places. ("A Country Love Story" bears an interesting relationship to a very late story of Jean Stafford's, "Lives of the Poets," published in 1978.)

One cannot quarrel with the prevailing critical assessment that finds Jean Stafford's art "poised," "highly reflective," "fastidious," "feminine." And certainly she worked within the dominant fictional mode or consciousness of her time—there are no experimental tales in the *Collected Stories* (which cover the years 1944–69); no explorations beyond the Jamesian-Chekhovian-Joycean model in which most "literary" writers wrote during those years. (Joycean, that is, in terms of *Dubliners* alone.) Each story remains within the consciousness of an intelligent and highly sensitive observer who assembles details from the present and summons forth details from the past, usually with a graceful, urbane irony; each story moves toward an "epiphany," usually in the very last sentence. There is very little that remains mysterious in Stafford's stories, little that is perplexing or disturbing in terms of technique, structure, or style. Some of the stories, it must be admitted, are marred by an arch, overwritten self-consciousness, too elaborate, too artificial, to have arisen naturally from the fable at hand (as in "I Love Someone," "Children Are Bored on Sunday," "The Captain's Gift"). Characters tend to resemble one another in speech and manners, and there is little distinction between men and women; occasionally the author offers clichés in place of careful observation—Beatrice Trueblood's neighborhood in New York City, for instance, is quickly assembled along the lines of a stage setting: there are rowdy street urchins, a bloody-faced "bum" on the sidewalk, brick façades of "odious mustardy brown."

When one considers the finest of the stories, however, one is impressed by the rigorous structure that underlies the "beautiful" prose. And there are of course sudden jarring images, sudden reversals, that brilliantly challenge the sensibility evoked by the fiction's near-constant authorial voice—which is, for the most part, reflective, obsessively analytical, compulsively self-conscious. Consider the brutal yet lighthearted—and charming!—Dr. Reinmuth of "The Maiden," offering as a dinner-table anecdote in postwar Heidelberg the story of how, invigorated by a guillotining he saw at the age of twenty-three, he rushed to propose to his presumably genteel German sweetheart. (Astonishing his fellow guests with his recollection of the guillotining, Dr. Reinmuth says zestfully: "One, he was horizontal! Two, the blade descended! Three, the head was off the carcass and the blood shot out from the neck like a volcano, a geyser, the flame from an explosion. . . . I did not faint. You remember that this was a beautiful day in spring? And that I was a young man, all dressed up at seven in the morning? . . . I took the train to Fürth and I called my sweetheart. . . . 'I know it's an unusual time of day to call, but I have something unusual to say. Will you marry me?' ") Consider the vicious killing of Shannon, the monkey, by Gran's "watchdog" (and alter ego) Caesar of "In the Zoo"; and Caesar's protracted death-agonies when, next day, he is poisoned by Shannon's grieving owner. Less dramatic, perhaps, but no less cruel, is the haircut poor little Hannah must endure, as part of the ongoing duel of wife and husband in "Cops and Robbers," one of the most successful of the stories. The most startling image in all of Stafford's fiction is the "perfectly cooked baby"—a black baby, of course—offered to the racist Sundstrom by a similarly racist friend in "A Modest Proposal": "It was charred on the outside, naturally, but I knew it was bound to be sweet and tender inside. So I took him home . . . and told [Sundstrom] to come along for dinner. I heated the toddler up and put him on a platter and garnished him with parsley . . . and you never saw a tastier dish in your life. . . . And what do you think he did after all the trouble I'd gone to? Refused to eat any of it, the sentimentalist! And *he* called *me* a cannibal!" (It is one of the ironies of "A Modest Proposal" that the reader never learns whether the incident ever happened, or whether the speaker has been telling a tall tale to upset the captain's guests.)

Subdued and analytical and beautifully constructed stories, then, in what might be called a "conventional" fictional mode: but they are not to be too quickly grasped, too glibly assessed. The "interior castle" of Stafford's art is one which will repay close scrutiny, for its meanings open slowly outward, and each phrase, each word, is deliberately chosen. Consider, for instance, the terrifying yet rigorously controlled conclusion of Pansy Vanneman's parablelike story: "The knives ground and carved and curried and scoured the wounds they made; the scissors clipped hard gristle and the scalpels chipped off bone. It was as if a tangle of tiny nerves were being cut dexterously, one by one; the pain writhed spirally and came to her who was a pink bird and sat on the top of a cone. The pain was a pyramid made of a diamond; it was an intense light; it was the hottest fire, the coldest chill, the highest peak, the fastest force, the furthest reach, the newest time. It possessed nothing of her but its one infinitesimal scene: beyond the screen as thin as gossamer, the brain trembled for its life. . . ." After the operation Pansy knows herself violated, her interior castle plundered; she is both healing, and doomed. She lies unmoving "as if in a hammock in a pause of bitterness. She closed her eyes, shutting herself up within her treasureless head."

Before God Was Love

THE SHORT STORIES OF
PAUL BOWLES

Thirty-nine stories, coldly and impeccably crafted, the work of four decades: tales set, for the most part, in Morocco, Mexico, and South America, in landscapes of a superlunary authority. (Even Bowles's Manhattan is not our Manhattan.) To state that the intensely evoked settings of Bowles's disturbing stories are usually hostile to his people—natives as well as hapless North Americans—is perhaps misleading, for the setting of a typical Bowles story possesses more life, more identity, than the human beings who find themselves trapped in it, succumbing to fates that read more like ominous parables than "stories" in the usual sense of the word. In one of his poems D. H. Lawrence speaks of a creature whose origins predate not only man, but God—a creature born "before God was love"—

Paul Bowles, *The Collected Stories of Paul Bowles,* 1939–1976 (Santa Barbara, California: Black Sparrow Press, 1979).

and it is precisely this sense of a natural world predating and excluding consciousness that Paul Bowles dramatizes so powerfully in his fiction. It is not an accident that the doomed professor (of linguistics) of the notorious story "A Distant Episode" loses his tongue before he loses his sanity, and his humanity, a captive of an outlaw tribe of the Sahara; nor is it chance that the American girl Aileen, visiting her mother and her mother's Lesbian-companion in Colombia, in "The Echo," succumbs to an irrational violence more alarming than any she has witnessed, and, while attacking her mother's lover, "uttered the greatest scream of her life"—pure sound, bestial and liberating.

Too much has been made, perhaps, of the dreamlike brutality of Bowles's imagination, which evokes a horror far more persuasive than anything in Poe, or in Gide (whom Bowles peripherally resembles). But the stories, like fairy tales, tend to dissolve into their elements because so little that is "human" in a psychological sense is given. The reader is usually outside Bowles's characters, even in those stories—"You Are Not I," "Pages from Cold Point," "Reminders of Bouselham"—in which a first-person narrator speaks. Most of the stories are terrible without being terrifying, as if the events they delineate take place outside our customary human world. A young boy is tortured and castrated in the desert by a maddened hashish smoker ("The Delicate Prey"); an Amazonian woman, living in a squalid ruin in Mexico, captures infants in order to devour their hearts and thereby gain supernatural power ("Doña Faustina"); the soul of a kif-besotted boy passes into a snake who has "the joy of pushing his fangs" into two men before he is killed ("Allal"); a sensitive young Mexican girl succumbs to the atmosphere of sadism about her, and accepts a kinship with "monstrous" spiders who live in the crevices of her bedroom wall ("At Paso Rojo"). In "Call at Corazón" a traveler abandons his alcoholic wife to an unimaginable fate in the South American jungle; in "The Hours After Noon" a child molester is driven by a fellow European into the Moroccan hills, where his fate (a few twists of wire about the neck) is inevitable, once he approaches an Arab child. The last we see of the North

American professor of linguistics he has become sheer animal: ". . . Bellowing as loud as he could, he attacked the house and its belongings. Then he attacked the door into the street. . . . He climbed through the opening . . . and still bellowing and shaking his arms in the air . . . he began to gallop along the quiet street toward the gateway of the town. A few people looked at him with great curiosity." A soldier shoots at him, idly, and he runs in terror out into the desert, into "the great silence out there beyond the gate." The insight of Conrad's Kurtz—"The horror! The horror!"—strikes a reader fresh from Bowles's fiction as supremely romantic, even sentimental. Conrad's Africa remains comfortingly European: its terrors can be verbalized.

Even those stories in which nothing explicitly violent occurs, stories which would probably not offend the average genteel reader—"The Frozen Fields," "The Time of Friendship"—create an unnerving suspense by virtue of Bowles's masterly craft. He has learned from Hemingway as well as Lawrence; even his descriptions are wonderfully dramatic. Nothing is extraneous, nothing is wasted. If one wants, at times, more humanity—more "consciousness"— surely this is a naïve prejudice, a wish that art affirm our human vantage point, as if the brute implacable *otherness* of the natural world were no more threatening than a painted backdrop for an adventure film. Though Bowles's marvelous landscapes call to mind another twentieth-century master of short fiction, D. H. Lawrence, it is misleading to read Bowles in the light of Lawrence. Even in Lawrence's coldest, most "legendary" tales, where landscape overcomes humanity—"The Man Who Loved Islands," "The Woman Who Rode Away"—one confronts and, to some extent, lives within recognizable human beings whose personalities are always convincing; and this is not true in Bowles. Lawrence's people are like us, Bowles's people tend to be our very distant kin, shadowy and remote, unclaimable. One cannot imagine Bowles creating a Constance Chatterly or a Mellors, trembling with apprehension of each other, or a Gerald (of *Woman in Love*), so susceptible to erotic passion that he chooses death rather than a life without the woman he desires. Desire in Bowles's fiction—in "Under the Sky," for instance, where a Mexican peasant rapes an American woman—is no more articulated than the emotion of the deranged professor of linguistics. Bowles does not write of sexual love in order to challenge its mythology, like many contemporary writers; he does not write about it at all. His interests lie elsewhere.

This collection, a companion to *The Thicket of Spring* (1972), which brought together four decades of Bowles's poetry, should strengthen Paul Bowles's position in American literature. Austere, remorseless, always beautifully crafted, the best of these stories are bleakly unconsoling as the immense deserts about which Bowles writes with such power, and they linger in the memory—disturbing, vexing—literally for decades. The reader is advised to approach them with caution, however, limiting himself to one or two at a sitting. For these are stories set in an epoch "before God was love," and beside them most acclaimed fiction of our time—brightly and nervously ironic, or dutifully attuned to the latest "moral" problems—seems merely shallow.

Colette's Purgatory

The wily lunatic is lost if through the narrowest crack
he allows a sane eye to peer into his locked universe and
thus profane it.

—COLETTE

In the eccentric volume of reminiscences and speculation Colette published in 1932, *The Pure and the Impure* (originally titled *Ces Plaisirs* . . .), there is a passage in which Colette speaks of the child hidden in the heart of every professional writer: "a child obstinately infatuated with technique, flaunting the tricks and wiles of his trade." One of the characteristics of Colette's writing has always been its seductive nature. Her style, even in translation, is a curious achievement: sensuous, yet analytical; elliptical, allusive, "poetic," and yet extraordinarily frank. If she was concerned with theatrical personalities and with certain flamboyant members of the Parisian demimonde it was perhaps as a consequence of her recognition of the

Colette, *The Other One*. Translated by Roger Senhouse and Elizabeth Tait (New York: Farrar, Straus & Giroux, 1977).
Colette, *The Blue Lantern,* Translated by Roger Senhouse (New York: Farrar, Straus & Giroux, 1963).

writer's kinship with such "professionals." She did not imagine herself superior to her subjects, she did not set herself apart from them in judgment; except for passages in the concluding pages of her masterpiece, *The Last of Chérie,* in which one can glimpse a political and social world *out there,* beyond the airless, claustrophobic, and doomed world of Chérie's narcissism, there is remarkably little sense in Colette of a moral dimension that might deal with her characters rigorously or cruelly. If men commit suicide in Colette's work—like Chérie, like Michel of *Duo,* like one of the unfortunate homosexuals of *The Pure and the Impure*—it is never because they realize their uselessness as human beings, but only because of thwarted love. And even then it is not "love" that destroys so much as the melancholy recognition of love's illusory nature.

That Colette should have identified with imposture of various types is not surprising. Married to the manic Willy, a self-proclaimed literary genius who was unfortunately unable to write, and who hired a stable of "secretaries" to write his books for him, she became a writer (according to her own account) only because her husband was pressed for money; she was his most talented "ghost" and it was to be many years before she could claim her own books, producing, after Willy's death, the original schoolgirl's notebooks in which she wrote the Claudine novels. Would she have become a writer otherwise? Would she have become "Colette" had there been no "Willy"? Still more astonishing is her defense of her father, another self-proclaimed writer who wrote nothing at all. In *Earthly Paradise* Colette speaks kindly of him as a born writer who left little work behind; in fact it was discovered after his death that the dozen volumes of his "writing"—each containing as many as three hundred pages—were composed of entirely blank pages, beautiful, thick, carefully trimmed papers. This was the "spiritual legacy," Colette claims, which she drew upon when she began to write under her husband's guidance!

The Other One, originally published in 1929 (as *La Seconde*), is not so striking an accomplishment as *The End of Chérie* (of 1926), nor has it the sensuous yet curiously elegiac beauty of *The Ripening Seed* (*Le Blé en herbe* of 1923); yet it is a considerable achievement nevertheless. Light, deft, rueful rather than ironic, *The Other One* explores the shifting network of relationships that constitute a household dominated by a successful Parisian playwright named Farou. He has been married for more than a decade to a handsome, plump, rather lazy woman named Fanny who has allowed him any number of casual mistresses and who has not *seemed* to mind his infidelities; but when it is revealed to Fanny (by her teenaged stepson) that he is having a love affair with the young woman who lives with them as his secretary, and Fanny's intimate companion, she becomes uncharacteristically upset. Fanny discovers that it is not inevitable that two women must compete for a man's affections; she discovers, to her surprise, that she has become as dependent upon the young woman, Jane, as her husband himself. In fact she may be fonder of Jane than Farou is. Distraught, bewildered, she comes to the conclusion that while Farou could replace his mistress within a week she, Fanny, cannot so easily replace a close friend. And the prospect of living alone with her husband alarms her. "Two of us"— that is, two women—"are not too many to be alone with Farou—to stand up to Farou," she thinks.

Chérie kills himself not only because his former mistress Léa has grown old, and quite cheerfully old, but because he discovers that he had been, in the course of *her* promiscuous career, only one young man among a veritable army; Michel of *Duo* kills himself because his wife of a decade has committed adultery and he cannot forgive her, or forget the terms of her infidelity. Fanny, who has no identity beyond her role as a famous playwright's wife, and who has not even had a child of her own, might very well have drifted into depression and finally into suicide, but she is saved by her affection—or love— for her husband's attractive mistress. If she had succumbed to jealousy she would have been destroyed: a brief illness, however, finds her philosophical about her predicament and about the predicament of women generally. Considering marriage, she thinks of the couples she and Farou knows and tries to assess how large a share of a man women can get for themselves, and comes to the conclusion that it is a fairly small one. Does it matter? Is it so very important?

Perhaps it is only a woman's pride that is damaged. Marriage is a sort of masquerade, a dance of impostors who flaunt the "tricks and wiles" of their roles, and perhaps the crucial issue is not fidelity itself so much as an ability—an enthusiastic ability—to sustain the imposture.

Refusing to be destroyed by her husband's unfaithfulness, Fanny is allowed a disturbing insight, one which Colette presents with absolute seriousness. She repudiates the "pure religion" in favor of a more congenial, and more realistic, solution to the problem of infidelity in marriage: her heroine "turned again to the help which could spring only from an alliance, even if it was uncertain and slightly disloyal, from a feminine alliance, constantly broken by the man and constantly re-established at the man's expense. . . ." Unlike the homosexual relationship between Claudine and her husband's secret mistress Rézi, explored in some detail in *The Indulgent Husband (Claudine en ménage),* this relationship is one of friendship and companionship, an alliance against male hypocrisy. The Other One would seem to refer to Jane, Farou's mistress; but perhaps in a more subtle way it refers to Farou himself. Wife and mistress recognize their common bond—or common victimization—and achieve a depth of affection possibly not available to men.

Colette's disillusion with romantic love began almost immediately after her marriage to Willy, who was fifteen years older than she and widely experienced in the superficial, breezy, "sophisticated" manner of Farou and of Renaud, Claudine's *mari-papa;* though Colette treats adolescents sympathetically (the portrait of Philippe of *The Ripening Seed* is a particularly moving one), she is often quite contemptuous of adult men. Not that they are malicious, or willfully perverse: they are simply incapable of fidelity. As a young girl Colette discovered the tragic disparity between happiness—or the illusion of happiness—and its absence, "between love and the laborious, exhausting pastime of sex" *(Earthly Paradise)* and even her lighter novels, like *The Other One,* are qualified by this melancholy insight.

What a melancholy burden, the yearning, the need, to ceaselessly appease these pleasures one calls *merely* physical . . .! To the sensualist the body becomes a duty; and as all love affairs tend to create a dead-end atmosphere, the lover finds himself in a hell of his own making, in what Colette calls, wittily, a "gymnast's purgatory." Though Colette herself strikes us as a marvelously eccentric person, her characterizations curve toward the representative, the universal, all the more as they illustrate the perverse burdens of love. A famous lover assures Colette in *The Pure and the Impure* that it is indispensable to make love, but only with women to whom he feels indifferent. In denying the selfhood of others he denies himself; he ceases to exist except as an aging obsessive Don Juan. Even in *The Ripening Seed* poor Vinca, beleaguered by passions she cannot understand, speaks quite out of character in crying to her young lover: "Don't you realize I know as much as the first woman God created?" And Colette says of the lovers, dispassionately, rather clinically:

> Phil misinterpreted the will-to-survive vested in the female of every species, and the imperious instinct to wallow in calamity while at the same time working it like a mine rich in precious ore. Abetted by the evening hour and his own fatigue, he felt exasperated by this combative chit, battling as she was in her primitive way for the preservation of their united future.

At the extreme poles of Male and Female we dissolve, evidently, into instinct; we become "primitive"—even allegorical. Colette tells us that Damien rejects her because she isn't quite a woman. Though she has tried systematically to rid herself of "ambiguity," there is a masculine streak (her will? her intelligence? her eccentricity itself?) that cannot be eradicated. And how fortunate for Colette the artist that this ambiguity is never resolved, and that she never wallows in the instinctive certainties of little Vinca!

The Blue Lantern was originally published in 1949 under the title *Le Fanal bleu*. It is a superbly documented journal of a Colette "dulled with age," crippled with arthritis, yet remarkably attuned to the sensuous details of ordinary life, and informed with an ironic detachment that allows no self-pity and not even an invalid's pride in the absence of self-pity. "I ride at anchor," Colette states, "beneath the blue lantern, which is quite simply a powerful commercial lamp at the end of a lengthy extensible arm, fitted with a blue bulb and a blue paper shade." A vivid symbol of the imagination, the blue lantern is never offered as a symbol; nor are the frequently heartbreaking details of an invalid's life offered to us as anything other than "ordinary." Between the ages of seventy-three and seventy-five Colette made use of her bouts of insomnia by writing in this journal, recording her impressions of Geneva after the war, and of the younger generation (with whom she feels frequently uneasy), and of the distressing animality and brutality that characterized certain Parisian children, conditioned by the war to "jungle practices." She reminisces, recalling her many beloved friends who have died, among them the actress Marguerite Moreno; she records conversations with Jean Cocteau, who like herself suffered an attack of "radio fright" during a broadcast; she includes a half-dozen letters from admirers and would-be writers and the merely curious and impertinent, wondering in what spirit such letters should be read: "Is there anything to be found in them other than calm self-assurance, with above all an astounding ignorance of real life and, in contradistinction, the secret cult of the self and the crying need for publicity?"

The Blue Lantern is perhaps not so rich an autobiographical work as the various reminiscences that make up *Earthly Paradise,* but it is beautifully translated by Roger Senhouse and is, for its length, an unforgettable record of that state of uneasy vigilance imposed upon an invalid by sheer physical pain and dread of further pain. Beneath the blue lantern, Colette says, her lifeline grows ever shorter and shorter, and she has become, herself, the text of her own sermon: discovering to her astonishment that her senses are atrophying and that even pain must be valued because it is symptomatic of life. An old woman, she is determined not to succumb to age, and yet she is even more determined not to play at being young. "In anticipation of the time when I shall no longer be able to move," Colette says, "I make no effort to move." Though in her own words the journal throws no light on events significant enough to astonish, it nevertheless has the power to deeply move, and to awaken in us a frightened sympathy for the plight of the aged and the crippled, and those who sense themselves soon to die (though in fact Colette was not to die until 1954): "Instead, then, of landing on new islands of discovery, is my course set for the open sea where there is no sound other than that of the lonely heart-beat comparable to the pounding of the surf? Rest assured, nothing is decaying, it is I who am drifting. . . . The open sea, but not the wilderness. The discovery that there is no wilderness! That in itself is enough to sustain me in triumphing over my afflictions."

In a sense she knows herself immortal, even as her hand begins to tremble. She knows herself beyond the "tricks and wiles" of imposture, having discovered that so long as she lives she will write—something in her will demands its expression. In all humility she recognizes the fact that for her there is no other destiny.

> When does writing have an end? What is the warning sign? A trembling of the hand? I used to think that it was the same with the completed book as with other finished ploys, you down tools and raise the joyful cry "Finished!," then you clap your hands only to find pouring from them grains of sand you believed to be precious. That is the moment when, in the figures inscribed by those grains of sand, you may read the words "To be continued. . . ."

The great theme of Colette's work is the tragedy of mutability: the innocent, brutal delight all lovers take in sensual pleasure, and the broken and bewildered aftermath of that pleasure when it becomes clear that what has been so passionately worshipped is, if not illusory, ruthlessly ephemeral. Human beings do not possess beauty but are possessed by it, as precarious in their substance as the play of sunlight and shadow upon one of Colette's meticulously observed landscapes. The most haunting beauty owes its genesis (and its inhuman power) to the imagination that dwells upon it, for the lover is a kind of artist, endowing his beloved with qualities not his own; and as the yearning soul of the lover is projected onto and defined by the beloved, so is human happiness bound up with that feat of the imagination that surpasses any activity of conscious will. It is appropriate, then, that the artist Colette—who has spoken of herself as psychologically bisexual in *The Pure and the Impure,* half-complaining of a "genuine mental hermaphroditism which burdens certain highly complex human beings"—should come to see herself finally as not only asexual but curiously and profoundly selfless: no longer burdened by the "intractable, lordly senses" she has praised and feared throughout her life but illuminated by a destiny she could not have anticipated, and surely could not have denied.

Géza Csáth's Garden

THE CONTOURS OF SURREALISM

Though allegory and Surrealism share a surface similarity, evoking dream worlds that violate the laws of the "real" world, it must be remembered that their motives differ radically. Allegory points outward, to a presumably communal tradition; Surrealism exults in the inward, the defiantly idiosyncratic and perverse. The allegorical artist's impulse is didactic while the Surrealist may wish to do nothing more—but isn't this everything?—than to celebrate the claustrophilia of the imagination. Details are magnified, and monstrous; or perhaps they are comic; in any case their effect is unsettling, because they rarely coalesce into a whole. The texture of sentences—of individual words—becomes extremely important, precisely as "meaning" is abandoned. The outer world is surrendered to

Géza Csáth's *The Magician's Garden and Other Stories* (New York: Columbia University Press, 1980).

naturalistic writers, or to journalists; hallucinations take on the religious sanctity of visions; one burrows more and more deeply— and more obsessively—into oneself, frantic to escape what the Hungarian Modernist Géza Csáth calls the "boring monotony of life's bullying rhythms."

Though the temperament of the Surrealist is often adolescent, or even prepubescent, his passion for dramatic extremes gives to his art, at least immediately, an uncanny authority frequently denied the more mature and more reasonable artist. Surrealist writing always strikes the intimate and somewhat shameful note of confession, for the Surrealist, locked into his narcissism, either cannot or refuses to objectify his experience. He will not cultivate a mask, he *will* speak directly. His contempt for what we call the "real" world is so profound that he rarely condescends to mention it. Nothing *out there* exists with any authority, so that one must turn inward, mesmerized by one's own dreams (whether ecstatic visions or hideous night- mares), eager to surrender one's place in history. If a prolonged immersion in art will not produce a sufficient derangement of the senses one is obliged—like Baudelaire, Huysmans, Rimbaud, and many others—to experiment with drugs. Though he is not to be defined as a Surrealist, Flaubert surely spoke for all Surrealists in saying, "Life is such a hideous business that the only method of bearing it is to avoid it. And one does avoid it by living in Art."

If Kafka tends to remain our touchstone so far as Surrealist fiction is concerned, this is hardly more than a measure of our general ignorance of the kinds of experimental writing that were being done in the first decades of the twentieth century. Géza Csáth, for instance, wrote his outstanding work between 1908 and 1912; his depiction of the collapse of Central Europe, by way of a delirious magnification of the collapse of the individual—the "magician" in particular—is uncannily prophetic. The fusing of a Kafkaesque world-vision with the language of a rapturous hedonism: this gives some indication, however oblique, of Csáth's curious talent.

Like most obsessive Surrealists Csáth is unevenly effective. *The Magician's Garden* is frequently blurred and sketchy, as if written without revision, and overburdened with an excess of dream-detail; yet its whole far exceeds the sum of its parts, and the stylish illustrations in the manner of Beardsley by Csáth's artist-friend Atilla Sassy (whose *Opium Dreams* sequence of 1909 was as controversial as Csáth's fiction) do much to enforce the atmosphere of mordant lushness. The volume is given another—quite unintended—significance when it is studied in the light of Csáth's tragic personal life, since one can read it, for all its drunken heterogeneity, as if it constituted an autobiographical novel. For though it is probably true that the narcissist, glorying in his insularity, would scorn the critic's predilection for seeing cultural meanings in the deliberately private and subjective, we can read Csáth's almost unrelievedly pessimistic fiction as representative of the spirit—if not the actual public voice— of a dying bourgeois order. Csáth's persona, the magician who dies young (at the age of twenty-nine) because he prefers opium to everything the world offers—even the love of a pure, sweet, selfless dream-woman—is perhaps not so private a creation as he might have thought. As we know, there are many kinds of opium, many ways in initiating a protracted suicide.

The Magician's Garden contains twenty-four prose pieces, some of them mere dream-sketches of little interest in themselves (the imagery of Csáth's typical dream is far less arresting, less individual, than that of Kafka's, for instance: there is a Technicolor lushness to the opium dream that can soon become tedious), some of them fairly long and complex stories that exhibit a surprising range of styles— from the chillingly atonic to the mesmerizing and incantatory. There is a marvelous Chekhovian story called "Murder" in which the alarming "bestial pleasure of killing" is explored in straightforward language (a rich landowner's son strangles one of his father's impoverished peasants); there is the brutal realism of "Trepov on the Dissecting Table" in which a corpse is cheerfully beaten by two orderlies; there are dream-heavy poetic excursions into secret gardens which contain, not surprisingly, images as terrifying as those of the real world. "Matricide" tells in uninflected prose the story of a middle-class woman murdered by her two teenaged sons, who show absolutely no remorse afterward. "Little Emma" depicts the almost incidental hanging of an unusually beautiful child by her sadistic playmates. "Meeting Mother" is a touchingly sentimental and presumably autobiographical sketch about a dream-encounter with the narrator's young mother, who died giving birth to him. (In fact Csáth's mother died when he was nine.) Though there are arresting moments in most of the fantasies, it is the naturalistic pieces—the passionate little essay "Opium" in particular—that are the most compelling. Csáth's exploration of his motives as a "pale greedy neurotic" who gladly surrendered decades of his life in exchange for the seductive hallucinations of opium tells us as much in three or four pages as we might get from an entire volume by Huysmans.

Csáth's personal history is remarkable. He was so precocious that he not only began to publish fiction at the age of sixteen, but he was evidently considered one of the "promises" of modern Hungarian prose. He was also highly gifted as an artist and a musician (his father wanted him to become a concert violinist). He enrolled in medical school, however, specialized in neurology, and published what was considered a major monograph (appropriately, *On the Psychic Mechanism of Mental Disorder*) in his mid-twenties. At the same time he was writing his fiction and publishing in the most important literary journals in Hungary, and became known as a particularly astute music critic (he was one of the first to appreciate the music of Bartók and Kodály). A prodigious talent, possessed of an extraordinary drive and energy—yet already an opium addict (he began taking opium at the age of twenty-two) with no more than a decade to live.

The Magician's Garden, taken as a whole, as a sort of impressionistic diary of Csáth's unhappy and truncated life, does not exactly dispel the mystery of the young man's choice of what he calls a slow suicide, but it allows us to overhear him talking to himself, obsessively and defiantly, about the nature of that choice. (Which was wholly conscious. Csáth knew exactly what opium would do to him.) Like so many gifted poets and writers of his time—of any time, no doubt—Csáth was both blessed and cursed by a sort of hyperesthesia of the spirit. He *knew* so much, he *saw* so much—how could he act? Lethargic, passive, "insolently lazy," incapable of loving anyone (he made a blatantly unwise marriage and eventually shot his wife with a revolver, in the presence of their infant daughter), he turns greedily inward, besotted with his own debilitating dreams. One thinks of Flaubert's decision for Art (as an "ascetic" religion); one thinks of Max Ernst's epiphany (as he leafed idly through an advertising catalog, in 1919) in which a sudden intensification of his "visionary faculties" brought forth a sense of the absurd so violent that he immediately embarked upon a series of drawings and paintings to express it—intent only upon reproducing what seemed to *see itself in him,* to use Ernst's phrase. Hallucination, or vision? Art is an insatiable devourer, making no distinctions. At such moments in the individual's history and in the history of his art it is the creative impulse itself that seems to insist upon expression, quite empty of moral content.

In "Opium" Csáth explains:

> Our face in the mirror reflects mere shapeless, stiff blotchings that have nothing to do with us, obviously. Trains pull into stations and people and horse-drawn carriages trot past in the streets. How marvelous all that is, and conducive to suffering; at the same time strange, incomprehensible, leading to the conviction that in their present forms things have neither reason nor purpose. Hence one must escape. . . . Pleasure erases contours, dissolves senselessness, freeing us from the shackles of space, halting the rattling of the clock's seconds; it lifts us on its sultry undulations to the highest reaches of Life.

Though opium eventually destroys the organs and senses it is nevertheless "blessed": health, after all, is bourgeois. If one can devote fourteen hours a day to opium, one should, without hesitation, for in a single day one can live thousands of years. One can transcend time—and to Csáth the passage of time is the single incontestable horror in life. Csáth's decision for opium (and slow suicide, though his own deterioration came more rapidly than he could have anticipated), so meticulously argued, is characteristic of decadent literature in general. Huysmans and Wilde, for instance, impress us with the rhetorical *orderliness* of their arguments for disorder. Nothing matters except interior sensation. Unless, of course, it is the verbal expression of that sensation—and some measure of fame or notoriety in the "real world" that is being rejected.

Still, one wants to rescue the vision itself—or at least to confirm its authenticity as an inevitable human response, necessary (so it appears) at certain moments in history. Csáth's Austro-Hungarian empire—Baudelaire's France—Wilde's England—the America of Poe—are these worlds that destroy only the weak, or is it a matter of some curious sort of strength (covert, stubborn, sly) that the "victim" defines himself triumphantly against them? Suicide is inescapably a political act, though rarely acknowledged as such.

At the same time *fin-de-siècle* speculations on the nature of reality and the role of the individual in this problematic reality strike a rather contemporary note. Surrealism is a technique, a shorthand, finally a poetic strategy by which the larger world is evoked—by implication. One is reminded, too, of Nietzsche's hypothesis in *Beyond Good and Evil* of 1886, which poses a question difficult to dismiss:

> Suppose nothing else were "given" as real except our world of desires and passions, and we could not get down, or up, to any other "reality" besides the reality of our drives—for thinking is merely a relation of these drives to each other: is it not permitted to make the experiment and to ask the question whether this "given" would not be *sufficient* for also understanding on the basis of this kind of thing the so-called mechanistic (or "material") world? I mean, not as a deception, as "mere appearance," an "idea" (in the sense of Berkeley and Schopenhauer) but as holding the same rank of reality as our affect—as a more primitive form of the world of affects in which everything still lies contained in a powerful unity . . . as a kind of instinctive life in which all organic functions are . . . intertwined—as a *pre-form* of life.

Nietzsche's speculation leads us into that bewildering cosmos in which everything is ordained and justified, and an individual's actions—even his withdrawal from all action—is contained within a great coherence. A religious affirmation without a reigning deity—not unlike the premoral Surrealist landscape in which both pleasure and pain "erase contours" and lift us (to use Csáth's hyperbolic prose) "to the highest reaches of Life."

"May God Grant That I Become Nothing"

THE MYSTICISM OF SIMONE WEIL

André Gide spoke of her as "the most spiritual writer of this century"; Albert Camus called her "the only great spirit of our time." T. S. Eliot seems to have been the first person to speak of her in terms of sainthood, declaring moreover that she was "a woman of genius." Weil herself, in speaking of the fallen condition of humanity *here below* (her curious expression for the phenomenal world), declared that in our present era it is not enough even to be a saint: "We must have the saintliness demanded by the present moment, a new saintliness, itself also without precedent."

Simone Weil had the apparent modesty to exempt herself from this "new saintliness" because she believed herself a hopeless sinner; in fact, she considered herself more reprehensible than the greatest of

Simone Weil, *The Simone Weil Reader,* edited by George A. Panichas (New York: David McKay Company, 1977).

criminals, for reasons that are not altogether clear. She set forth, however, with an air of remarkable authority, the means by which one might purify the self and approach the ultimate communion with God: which is to say, a systematic surrender of the world; a joyous acceptance of the Infinite; and an active embracing of the doctrine of "decreation" or "disincarnation." Weil's prayer echoes that of the ancient sect of Cathars, whom she admired above all orthodox followers of Christianity: "May God grant that I become nothing."

Since Catharism allowed for a form of indirect suicide by way of starvation, it is not surprising that Weil was attracted to its teachings. What more "saintly" project than to starve oneself to death in the ostensible service of a religious ideal? What more forthright and determined way to renounce the "fallen" world and the demanding flesh and the ubiquitous Devil?—and, not least, the torments of consciousness itself? No anorexic clinging defiantly to his or her representation of an ideal fleshless self has ever defined the terms of such saintliness (or delusion) more forcibly than Weil, in whom the instinct to die clearly preceded theory. In her impassioned essay "Decreation" she asserts that we can return to the divine only by way of "liberating" a trapped energy: and that this energy can be liberated only by actual death. "We must become nothing, we must go down to the vegetative level," Weil declares. "It is then that God becomes bread."

Weil the much-admired "saint," or Weil the self-deluded anorexic, possessed of a ferociously inviolate will even as she claims to possess no self: how is she to be judged, several decades after her death? Reading George A. Panichas's reverently edited collection of Simone Weil's writings, one is inclined to wonder if both Weil and her numerous admirers are not touched with a pernicious kind of madness: mad because Weil's "ideas" are so clearly without substance, mere vaporous and platitudinous musings; pernicious because, couched in an archetypal (or stereotypical) religious vocabulary, they cannot fail to exert a powerful appeal, even to the skeptic. Sacrifice, renunciation, asceticism, fasting, returning again to God (who then becomes "bread"): these are inclinations fueled as much by instinct as by religious idealism.

Then again, the puzzled reader thinks, is Weil speaking in parables? And is the body of her multifarious prose pieces really a kind of poem or extended metaphor, not to be taken literally? Weil herself, however, took it literally, and fasted to death in 1943, at the age of thirty-four, for political and religious reasons.

No one who knew Simone Weil could doubt that she was, from girlhood onward, an exceptional person. At least for some years she impressed observers as a brilliant and original thinker, in her long meditative essays "Analysis of Oppression," "The *Iliad,* Poem of Might," and "Uprootedness and Nationhood," in which she addressed, from a very different angle, those tragic aspects of contemporary civilization that so obsessed writers as dissimilar as D. H. Lawrence and Albert Camus. Weil seems to have believed that the social order in itself—perhaps because it is established *here below*—is intrinsically evil; and that there is a "diabolism" about the twentieth century in particular. Weil was clearly a person who came alive in conflict and combative argument: *give me something to oppose,* she might have said, *and I will know who I am.*

When Weil was twenty-eight years old, however, she experienced what might be called a conversion; and, after this, began to write passionately about religious and mystical matters. Retaining much of her authoritarian bias, and surrendering, it seems, virtually nothing of her misanthropic sentiments, she "discovers" the most remarkable of truths: God is love; appearance clings to being; God can only love Himself; affliction is the most precious evidence of God's "tenderness" for man; Christ is the key; all geometry proceeds from the Cross; all men bear an animal nature within them; life *here below* is sinful and fallen. Though Weil is often spoken of with reverence by liberals, she made it clear that, in her opinion, literature and "immorality" are inseparable and that literature should most certainly be censored—but only by "saints." Or, if no saints are forthcoming, by priests of the Roman Catholic Church who are empowered to speak for them.

Nietzsche speculated that the humble in spirit, the most adamantly "Christian" of persons, secretly wish to be exalted above their fellows and that their public humility is an inversion of their own thwarted will to power—or their timidity in claiming that will. Where humbleness is the characteristic pose, pride covertly reigns. The reiterated claim for selflessness is based upon the shaky proposition that such persons have underdeveloped or inferior selves: their spiritual "love" is really a form of resentment. ("A resentment experienced by creatures," Nietzsche says in *The Genealogy of Morals*, "who, deprived as they are of the proper outlet of action, are forced to find their compensation in an imaginary revenge." Hence, heaven is their proper abode; and hell that of their enemies.) Simone Weil's lifelong preoccupation with her "inferiority," her "worthlessness," her "sinfulness," does not contradict but in fact complements her inflated sense of knowing what God *really* intends for mankind.

According to the essay "A Spiritual Autobiography," Weil was so jealous of an older, and evidently brilliant, brother that she seriously thought of suicide, at least in theory, and became obsessed from that point onward with her characteristic attitude of rigorous self-loathing. The "resentment" of which Nietzsche speaks—and which, indeed, he saw as a central psychological reflex of Christianity in its orthodox forms—is closely linked with self-abasement and misdirected, or denied, anger. One affirms one's self by way of harsh denial: by way, in fact, of disintegration. "May God grant that I become nothing," the ascetic prays, as if to anticipate and, in a sense, overcome, the ineluctable plan of godless Nature that, with the simple passage of time, he *must* become nothing.

I will myself *not to be:* therefore, *I am*.

While Simone Weil's political essays are rigorously impersonal, those on other subjects, particularly religious experience, are punctuated by the motif of "inferiority." Weil flagellates herself as a "poor unsatisfactory creature," a "beggar," a "slave," a "worthless object." It is her hope that she will be sent to prison and might become impoverished. (She was born of a well-to-do Jewish family.) So filled with self-loathing is Weil that she cannot imagine the possibility that any human being could feel simple friendship, let alone love, for her.

Is it altogether surprising, then, that she one day discovers that God has, for His own inscrutable purpose, chosen *her* as a means by which His thoughts might be directly expressed, through the very pen she holds? A delicious paradox, absurdity with the true Kierkegaardian twist! "I would never dare speak to you like this if all these thoughts were the product of my own mind," Weil says to an acquaintance, in a letter of May 1942; but the thoughts are not Simone Weil's, of course: they are God's. And though Weil is a poor, unsatisfactory creature these thoughts, because they are God's and not hers, must be authentic. For, as Weil asserts, it does not matter if the consecrated host is made of the poorest quality of flour, not even if it is three parts rotten.

This phenomenon is all the more miraculous in that the vessel for God's wisdom knows herself unworthy of *that very salvation* she might aid others in attaining. As Weil remarks in a letter to a Catholic priest, her imagination, "mutilated by overlong and uninterrupted suffering," cannot conceive of salvation as a possibility for her. She alone is an outcast, a beggar, a slave. In fact, when she examines her conscience closely she is forced to the conclusion that she, more than any criminal, has just cause to fear God's wrath; for that would be a trivial sin in another person is a mortal sin in Weil.

This curious self-inflation is never questioned by any of Weil's admirers, who seem willing to accept her at her own estimation. In "A Spiritual Autobiography" even God becomes a participant in Weil's dramatization of the self, when, it seems, He deliberates for some time about whether Weil should be baptized in the Catholic Church and finally comes to the tentative conclusion that she should not. If God should change His mind, however, Weil would obey with alacrity. She would, in fact, "joyfully obey the order to go to the very center of hell and to remain there eternally." (Unless God is capricious or perverse, this is highly unlikely: for Weil is forced to admit that, after rigorous self-examination, she cannot discover any particular, *serious* faults in her behavior. And of course she has dedicated herself to a nunlike life of purity, for the very thought of carnal appetite is repulsive.)

God's magnificent anger, however, though it might be directed toward a faultless young woman who has suffered violent headaches and other disabilities without complaint for years, is not unjust or unwelcome—not at all. "By a strange twist," Weil says, "the thought of God's anger only arouses love in me." Affliction is, after all, a marvel of "divine technique." And though it is wrong to desire it one can be permitted to love its *possibility*. For, consider, our flesh is fragile; it can be pierced or torn or crushed, or one of its internal mechanisms can be permanently deranged, by any piece of matter in motion. We are not condemned, it seems, to eternal earthly happiness. Such is God's mercy that our fragility as creatures will ensure our decreation someday, and we may contemplate it with love and gratitude, stimulated by the occasion of "any suffering, whether great or small" ("The Love of God and Affliction"). It only seems that God is angry at us when we are afflicted or when thousands or millions of us are destroyed. In fact God loves us at such times. At such times, perhaps, more than others. Isn't our very misery proof of our special election? *"Malheur,"* says Weil, "is necessary so that the human creature may un-create itself."

Like Dostoyevsky Weil seems to have convinced herself that the suffering of mankind is an unqualified good, and woe to those who meddle with it. Imagine wanting to alter God's will . . . ! Isn't it a vicious sin, even, to feel sorry for sufferers? In a refugee camp in Casablanca Weil wrote that she sometimes felt moved when she saw afflicted people and that, for a certain space of time, her usual unqualified love of the merciful God was suspended; and this caused her grief because she must have offended God. "I hope he will forgive me my compassion," she says with absolute sincerity.

Yet is is doubtful that she was at heart a very compassionate person, or even a Christian in the usual sense of the word. She seems to have been charged with a self-righteous zeal that is, at times, rather chilling. In "The Responsibility of Writers" and "Morality and Literature" she blames writers of recent years for the disaster of the time—not only World War II but the "disaster" of the whole world so far as Western influence has penetrated. ("In recent years there have been some unbelievable degradations; for example, advice on love affairs by well-known writers. . . . Such easy morals in literature, such tolerance of baseness, involve our most eminent writers in responsibility for demoralizing country girls. . . .") Dadaism and Surrealism are, of course, totally unacceptable: they represent the "intoxication of license." But less extreme writers are equally guilty in undermining the morals of the time by their emphasis upon such qualities as spontaneity, sincerity, richness, etc., and their pointed ignoring of the age-old values of good and evil. Bergson is suspect in that he values Life itself; Proust is more concerned with beauty than with the Good; all "psychological" literature is reprehensible. In the seventeenth century, Weil asserts with approval, there were people with the "courage" to declare all writers immoral and to act upon their judgment, by sending them to prison or executing them.

It is not only imaginative literature, however, that is dangerous. It is the act of imagining itself. Daydreaming. And why is daydreaming so immoral? *Because it allows the afflicted person a respite from his condition and by such a way is God's will thwarted, however temporarily.* Only "reality," unsoftened by the wishes of a dreaming, yearning mind, is to be tolerated.

In the essay "Friendship" Weil states dogmatically that there can be no friendship when distance is not kept and respected. Erotic love is "unlawful" if the lovers imagine that they form a single entity; in fact, their relationship is "what might be called an adulterous union, even though it comes about between husband and wife." Elsewhere she speaks critically of carnal desires of all kinds (even hunger and thirst) because such desire is an orientation of the body toward the future, while a true detachment, an awareness of the "point of eternity" in one's soul, would be timeless. It is not surprising that Weil should speak with enthusiasm of the Gnostics, the Manichaeans, and the Cathars, and that she should speak contemptuously of the "coarseness of mind" that characterizes orthodox religion.

It has always been puzzling that Simone Weil's forthright anti-Semitism has been ignored, especially by her Jewish admirers. But how is it possible to extract her "saintliness" from her bigotry? The

most chilling single entry in *The Simone Weil Reader* is a letter of
November 1940 that Weil wrote to the French Ministry of Education, demanding her teaching job back because she did not consider
herself a Jew. (The Vichy government had recently passed a statute
denying the rights of Jews and persons of Jewish descent.) Step by
step, with a precise Kafkan logic, Weil takes up the popular defini-
tions of Judaism and declares herself outside them. She is careful not
to attack the statute itself; she is not at all concerned with her Jewish
colleagues' fate; she only wants to establish Simone Weil officially as a
non-Jew. Proudly and desperately she states: "Mine is the Christian,
French, Greek tradition. The Hebraic tradition is alien to me. . . . If,
nevertheless, the law insists that I consider the term, 'Jew,' whose
meaning I don't know, as applying to me, I am inclined to submit, as
I would to any law. . . . If the Statute does not apply to me, then I
should like to enjoy those rights which I am given by the contract
implied in my title of 'professor.' " One waits in vain for Weil to
protest the injustice of the statute, or to defend the rights of other
Jews who have been persecuted.

Despite Weil's mystical emphasis upon the "point of eternity,"
her life was characterized by furious bursts of energy. Born in Paris in
1909, to Jewish parents, she became involved at any early age with
Marxism, pacifism, and the trade union movement. Though evidently not temperamentally suited for teaching, she taught at various
girls' schools and even worked for a while in a factory—but was
dismissed for incompetence. She gave away most of her money to
"worthy" causes. Posing as a journalist, she joined the Republican
Front in the Spanish Civil War but was disabled after two months by
an accident, and later wrote a letter to Georges Bernanos denouncing
her former comrades for their cruelty. ("What do I care that you are a
royalist . . . ?" she asks. "You are incomparably nearer to me than my
comrades of the Aragon militias—and yet I loved them.") Increasingly disillusioned and embittered, and grown chronically ill, Weil
withdrew from an active involvement with the world and became
increasingly—and perhaps idiosyncratically—religious. She studied

Greek and Hindu philosophy and, in the years 1940–1942, engaged in intense mystical contemplation and fasting. Displaced by the war, she went to London in 1942, where, to protest the starvation of persons in German-occupied territories, she refused to eat; once hospitalized, she refused all medical treatment and nourishment; she died in 1943, at the age of thirty-four, of starvation and pulmonary tuberculosis, leaving behind a considerable oeuvre: eleven volumes of essays, notebooks, and letters on such subjects as philosophy, literature, history, art, classics, politics, education, economics, and religion. She seems to have known virtually everything; or, at the very least, to have had an opinion on it. The continuous posthumous publication of her works has assured her a place in twentieth-century letters, but it seems to be her mystical writings, and her self-determined death, that have made her famous.

If the essays are examined without reference to the life, however, they rarely rise above the commonplace. "Factory Work," for instance, suffers from its author's predilection for abstraction and analysis without regard for the specific: Weil shows virtually no interest in workers as members of families, as lovers or friends, as *human beings* with a multiplicity of identities and relationships. She is apparently ignorant of the writings of Dickens, Zola, and Lawrence, among others; and she makes no reference to other sociological studies of the effects of urban industrialization upon the "masses." In such essays as "Analysis of Oppression" and "Uprootedness and Nationhood," the possibility of individual happiness is never allowed: "mankind" is imagined as a sort of Platonic essence despoiled by an increasingly mechanized and organized state. (By contrast, see D. H. Lawrence's subtle discussion of the "bonding" between miners, in his little-known essay "Nottingham and the Mining Countryside," in *The New Adelphi*, June–August 1930.) "Reflections on the Right Use of School Studies" has been called by one of Weil's loyal admirers "marvelous foolishness of which one believes every word": but it is doubtful that we can take seriously an educational theory in which school studies of virtually any subject, *no matter how tedious or irrelevant,* might be employed as a means of acquiring the virtues of humility and attentiveness necessary to the love of God. Indeed, can any such theory be justified as "educational" at all? Even Weil's most famous essay, "The *Iliad*, Poem of Might," advances a relatively simple theory, which is expanded at great length: war is brutal and brutalizing. And Weil's concluding diatribe against what she sees as the "Roman" and the "Hebraic" influence in the West is shrilly unconvincing. The melancholy poetic vision of a great work is here made to yield to polemics.

As for Weil's famous mystical essays—"Beauty," "Contemplation of the Divine," "Last Thoughts," "A Spiritual Autobiography"— since they belong to that subspecies of literature Aldous Huxley has called the perennial philosophy, they do not differ in substance or in expression from the writings of numerous other mystics. Writing of the divine, one cannot be original unless, like Kafka or St. John of the Cross, one *is* original in his imagination. Otherwise, a Buddhist saint sounds very much like a Christian saint; Sufism speaks in the accents of the Maitrayana Upanishad; Eckhart and St. Theresa are brother and sister. And Weil, if one can judge fairly by these representative essays, sounds as if she has steeped herself in them all. Her vocabulary consists almost exclusively of nonreferential terms like *good* and *evil*, *beauty, eternity, the world, the divine, the universe, God*. Her early and abiding infatuation with Platonism underlies this predilection for the abstract at the expense of the specific, but since Weil is no poet, and evidently possessed a fairly limited imagination, her mystical writings are curiously argumentative and flat.

Now that much is known of Weil's life and her obsession with the mortification of the flesh (primarily by way of fasting), it is difficult to take her "visions" seriously. From the age of sixteen Weil evidently felt an extraordinary disgust for the physical life, which must have taken its secret revenge upon her in various ways: not least, in her susceptibility to conversion. She speaks of Christ in embarrassingly girlish terms, wondering if he loves her or not; at the age of twenty-nine, she was so deeply impressed by a young English Catholic (gifted with an "angelic radiance") that, not long afterward, Christ himself came to her one day and "possessed" her. She speaks frankly of the soul's "virginity" being taken by God, and of the soul's "sleeping with God." One of the most curious selections in the *Reader* is an hallucinatory sequence in which Christ comes to Weil like a lover. He is mysterious and abrupt and resolutely masculine. He gives her bread and wine (Weil has been systematically starving herself at this time); they stretch out on the floor together and sleep; they talk of various things, like old friends; then Christ drives her from him, for unclear reasons, and throws her out into the street. This unabashed masochistic fantasy was recorded during the last months of Weil's life, when she was in a severe and possibly irreversible anorexic state.

Virginia Woolf once said that unless she weighed a certain weight she saw visions and heard voices. Thus with us all. It is a fact of physiological life, as anyone who has experimented with fasting, even minimally, knows. At a certain point, simply by not eating, by assuming control of the body's "natural" appetite, one can experience both euphoria and a marvelous and unquestioned sense of certainty. Hence the grimly gloating obsession with starvation that character-izes the sufferer of anorexia nervosa: hence the inclination to "be-lieve" with great passion. (For, it seems, the skepticism of ordinary consciousness, as well as the psychological balance assured by a sense of humor, is lost in these odd "euphoric" states.) So light-headed, so exhausted, one is particularly susceptible to simple explanations of complex matters, and to the most extraordinary incursions from the unconscious: *Misery is joy. Death is life. Affliction is a blessing. God's cruelty assures His tenderness.* In this deranged state, induced by fasting and sleeplessness, Simone Weil made it a practice to repeat, continuously, the Lord's Prayer in Greek: with unsurprising "mysti-cal" results.

It has been said that Weil resembles Kafka's Hunger Artist. But the analogy is false, for Kafka's Artist dies with a realization of his own egoism and spite, and Simone Weil died with her defenses and delusions intact. She more accurately resembles D. H. Lawrence's autobiographical portrait of a Christlike figure in *The Escaped Cock*, who, before his graphic resurrection in the flesh, preached love for all of mankind while being incapable of touching, or tolerating the touch, of a single human being.

The contemporary reader is puzzled, finally, less by Weil herself than by the unquestioned loyalty of her admirers. Do they so crave "saintliness" (in others, if not in themselves) that they will transform a sick, desperate, broken woman into a model of spiritual health; do they so crave "wisdom" that they will accept the speculations of a greatly troubled mind as if these speculations were superior, in fact, to their own? Simone Weil's life and posthumous career are fascinating, and doubtless exemplary of the spiritual vacuum of our century: the hunger to believe in virtually anyone who makes a forthright claim to be divinely guided. *Here below*, we must make do with what we have.

Legendary Jung

There are many Jungs, and not simply because Carl Jung lived an unusually long and productive life. (He died in 1961, at the age of eighty-five, shortly after completing one of his least obscure essays, "Approaching the Unconscious.") There is the elderly, ailing man who says with convincing modesty, "I am astonished, disappointed, pleased with myself. I am distressed, depressed, rapturous. I am all these things at once, and cannot add up the sum. I am incapable of determining ultimate worth or worthlessness; I have no judgment about myself and my life. There is nothing I am quite sure about. I have no definite convictions—not about anything, really. I know only that I was born and exist. . . . I exist on the foundation of something I do not know." (From "Retrospect," in *Memories,*

C. G. Jung: Word and Image, edited by Aniela Jaffé (Princeton, N.J.: Princeton University Press, Series XCVII.2, 1979).

Dreams, Reflections.) There is the mythographer who shrewdly if perhaps not altogether consciously recasts his life as that of a hero—a Jungian hero—struggling and triumphing against innumerable dragons in the fulfillment of his "individuation," which is to say the completion of his soul; this is the elderly man who revenges himself upon a troubled and possibly disordered past by imposing a poet's sense of order upon it, imagining succinct dramatic scenes with Freud, among others, in which the best lines of dialogue are his, and the most compelling epiphanies. How *cannot* this legendary Jung succeed at whatever he attempts? "From the beginning," he says calmly, "I had a sense of destiny, as though my life was assigned to me by fate and had to be fulfilled. This gave me an inner security, and, though I could never prove it to myself, it proved itself to me. *I* did not have this certainty, it had me." (From "School Years," in *Memories, Dreams, Reflections.*) There is the brilliant young psychiatrist who enters upon a passionate, if largely epistolary, friendship with Sigmund Freud, offering himself to "our cause" (that is, the psychoanalytic revolution) though he has from the start serious misgivings about Freud's monomaniacal sexual pantheism, and knows very well that he is maneuvering himself (and the oddly masochistic Freud) into a false position: the younger man *will* boldly force the friendship to a violent end, yet he *will* suffer more than Freud from its dissolution. (See the *Freud/Jung Letters,* edited by William McGuire, Princeton/Bollingen Series XCIV: the "Freud" here created by Freud, and the "Jung" here created by Jung, are fascinating performers in a *folie à deux* of tragic proportions.) There is the devoted husband and father who nevertheless has an adulterous relationship with a former patient, Toni Wolff, that survives almost four decades—a heroic feat in itself—and who, while expressing distaste for anything so vulgar as gossip, worries aloud that future biographers will be unable to guess that he is a "great lover." (Jung's wife, Emma, and his mistress, Toni, acquired symbolic value in the Jungian cosmos, the former as the "wife and mother" whose identity resides in her domesticity, the latter the *"femme inspiratrice,"* or Muse, whose function is to stimulate the imagination of the man of genius.) There is the Jung who, in

1934, did not refrain from speaking against Freud's "subversive" Semitic psychoanalytic methodology. Yet there is the wise, kind, patient, sympathetic, and altogether admirable Jung revealed in the *Letters* (two volumes, edited by Gerhard Adler and Aniela Jaffé for the Bollingen Series), and there is, of course, the remarkable Jung, the incomparable Jung of the more than twenty volumes of *Collected Works*, certainly one of the most brilliant and disturbing thinkers of all time.

Carl Jung's works have been translated into English and published, one by one, since the early Fifties, by the Bollingen Foundation. There are handsome, and handsomely priced, hard-cover volumes like the volume under review; there are paperback editions (including a Viking Portable edited and annotated by Joseph Campbell); there are pious and unconvincing hagiographies like Laurens van der Post's *Jung and the Story of Our Time,* and near-scurrilous attacks like Paul J. Stern's *C. G. Jung: The Haunted Prophet,* which reads as if it had been written by Jung's impish shadow-self. There are richly detailed studies by Jungian analysts like June Singer *(Boundaries of the Soul),* and critical studies of literature employing Jungian methods of interpretation, varying widely in worth (one of the very finest in recent years, and a distinguished book of criticism in its own right, is Edward F. Edinger's *Melville's Moby Dick: "An American Nekyia");* there is Anthony Storr's lucid, intelligent *Jung.*

One has the impression that Jung is now widely and enthusiastically read. But by whom? Certain Jungian terms—*extravert, introvert, collective unconscious, archetype,* even *anima* and *animus* and *shadow*—are to be found virtually everywhere, in the most casual of contexts, employed by people who have never heard of, let alone made their heroic way through, such difficult works as *Aion, The Concept of the Collective Unconscious, Psychological Types,* or *Symbols of Transformation.* Academic psychology with its behaviorial foundations has no use for Jung, whose theories cannot be measured— cannot be proven or disproven; and even the brilliantly eclectic Julian Jaynes, whose *The Origins of Consciousness in the Breakdown of the Bicameral Mind* includes a massive bibliography, seems never to have read Jung. My academic and literary colleagues amaze me by the alacrity with which they dismiss Jung as obscure, or superficial, or mystical. Have you read Jung's study of the symbolism of the Mass? I inquire. Well—no. Have you read his essay on Eastern and Western ways of thinking, or his essay on poetry (which makes Freud's speculations on the same subject appear crudely naïve), or his masterpiece, *Answer to Job?* No, my colleagues admit, they haven't read these works. Nor have they read "The Phenomenology of the Spirit in Fairy Tales," or Jung's famous commentary on *The Secret of the Golden Flower;* they haven't even glanced through the elementary *Man and His Symbols.* Months later, or years later, we blunder onto the same topic. But haven't you read, yet—? I ask, dismayed. And the answer is, well—no, not yet.

C. G. Jung: Word and Image is a biographic—that is, a hagiographic—record of Jung's life and career. Based upon the 1975 centenary exhibit held in Zurich, and following more or less the self-dramatizing thematic outline of *Memories, Dreams, Reflections,* it is a problematic and yet a fascinating book. Much of the material is familiar (the relationship with Freud, the travels to North Africa, to the Pueblo Indians of New Mexico, to East Africa, and India), and a great deal of the text is simply taken from *Memories, Dreams, Reflections,* in truncated form; but the book contains much previously unpublished material, including eleven paintings from Jung's secret "Red Book," in which he transcribed inner experiences during the turbulent six-year period (1913–1919) following his break with Freud. And what astonishing paintings they are! As if Blake had attempted to portray his visions in Art Nouveau style—as if a gifted and precocious child had boldly delineated *his* interpretations of mystical Oriental art.

In 1913 Jung resigned his lecturership at the University of Zurich, and entered into his famous "confrontation with the unconscious." He did not resist visions, voices, obsessions, fantasies of a frequently terrifying nature; in order to reestablish contact with himself as a child, he played with building blocks, and labored to "translate emotions into images." Like Blake, who spoke of taking dictation from a source beyond himself, Jung wrote "in the style selected by the unconscious." He encountered dream-figures (among them an old wise man whom he called Philemon and who resembles, in the thirty-eight-year-old Jung's painting, the eighty-year-old Jung himself); he painted orange-red flames that billow up to the heavens, and a rodentlike "shadow-figure" in a gentleman's cape and high hat, and stylized serpents breathing fire, and apocalyptic crosses hovering above villages simple and flat as any imagined by Grandma Moses. He painted mandalas, one of which, "The Castle," is as labyrinthine as anything dreamt into being by Kafka. It was Jung's belief, which seems, judging from these illustrations, to be justified, that the dream visions were not products of the personal unconscious that might be traced back to biographical events; they were instead impersonal and mythic, arising out of a psychic realm to which Jung eventually gave the name "collective unconscious." Out of this six-year period came the *prima materia* for a life's work, which would carry Jung into the formidable (and unfashionable) fields of astrology, alchemy, and the occult. (Though in fact Jung's doctoral dissertation had been a study of "so-called occult phenomena.") Had Jung resisted the plummet into the unconscious, as most people do, he would not have made the discoveries for which he is famous—he would not have fulfilled the destiny "assigned" to him by fate.

C. G. Jung: Word and Image might have been strengthened by some judicious criticism of the Jung legend. It is, after all, a highly convincing Jungian thesis that any inflation of the ego, or of the ego's worldly reputation, will draw forth a counterstroke from the unconscious. For instance, one could not guess, judging from the book's final chapters, how certain of Jung's ideas (particularly those set forth with such courage and lucidity in *Answer to Job*) excited violently hostile responses from the very readers for whom it was intended. The continuing anti-Jungian bias of psychoanalysis might have been examined, for whatever it is worth. And one sees in two of the book's photographs (one at the famous Weimar Congress of 1911, the other at an Eranos lecture in the late Thirties) the melancholy figure of Toni Wolff, seated in both photographs just to the left of Emma

Jung, never identified as Jung's beloved and inordinately faithful *femme inspiratrice*. The book's weakest section is that given over to "Travels," since its illustrations are quite arbitrary and have nothing to do with Jung himself, and most of the commentary is taken directly from *Memories, Dreams, Reflections*. The funniest section is enlivened by quotes from Jung's letters to his wife, when he and Freud visited New York City in August of 1909, and suffered a mild sort of culture shock. (From which Freud never recovered: he spoke of the New World as a "gigantic mistake.") Jung writes Emma:

> We went to Brill's for supper. He has a nice, uncomplicated wife (an American). The meal was remarkable for the unbelievable, wildly imaginative dishes! Picture a salad made of apples, head lettuce, celery root, nuts, etc., etc. . . . Afterward, between 10 and 12 P.M., we drove down to Chinatown, the most dangerous part of New York. . . . The Chinese all wear dark clothing and have their hair in long braids. We went into a Chinese temple, located in a frightful den called a joss house. Around every corner a murder might be taking place. Then we went into a Chinese tea-house, where . . . they served us rice and an incredible dish with chopped meat, apparently smothered in earthworms and onions. . . . But the worms turned out to be Chinese potato. . . . By the way, the hoodlums who were lounging around looked more dangerous than the Chinese. In Chinatown there are 9,000 Chinese but only 28 women. . . . I should mention that Dr. Brill's wife was along for the whole expedition, like the good American she is.

For this, too, is Jung, unpremeditated and unmythologized.

Anne Sexton

SELF-PORTRAIT IN POETRY AND LETTERS

"My mouth blooms like a cut," the poet announces in a poem called "The Kiss." Her body has undergone a resurrection: her nerves are turned on, like musical instruments. "Where there was silence/the drums, the strings are incurably playing." A mysterious *you* is to account for the miracle. A "genius" of a lover, a composer, a carpenter, a man of many hearts. Does he exist, is he merely human? Mortal? In one incarnation he is the object of an adulterous passion, he is one half "of a pair of scissors/who come together to cut, without towels saying His. Hers" (from "Eighteen Days Without You"). In another incarnation he is distant and unfathomable, moving away, leaving his beloved "private in her breathbed" and placing her, like a phone, back on the hook. He has become God. God and lover have

Anne Sexton, *Love Poems,* (Boston: Houghton Mifflin, 1969); *The Awful Rowing Toward God,* (Boston: Houghton Mifflin, 1975); *A Self-Portrait in Letters* (Boston: Houghton Mifflin, 1977).

inexplicably fused. Love, which has drawn the poet out of her body, out of her deathly preoccupation with herself, has now failed, and the poet sinks back into the grave of herself. It is a miracle, too, of a kind.

Images of wounds, broken bones, blood, masks. The poems themselves are small angry wounds that bloom, blossom fiercely, like flowers, but, like flowers, have no strength, no permanency. Everything is provisional, no matter how ebullient, how joyful the poet's cry. "Your hand found mine," Sexton declares in "The Touch," and "Life rushed to my fingers like a blood clot." Is the imagery in this instance deliberately macabre, is it ironic—or merely a consequence of the poet's carelessness? No matter: life rushes to her fingers like a blood clot, and we know the role of blood clots in the body's history.

Sexton is the poet of ephemeral, dizzyingly ephemeral emotions. She is the poet of instantaneous moods. They are flicked before us like playing cards: now she is happy, now she is plunged into depression, now she is passionate and fulfilled, now she is empty, abandoned, ready to die. The obsession of her poetry as a whole is with the tragic limitations of this kind of life, the failure of the imagination to be equal to the demands of the soul, specifically the failure of the female to be equal to her exaggerated idea of herself: daughter but also mother, mother but also daughter, wife, beloved, "small jail," the woman who cries out "my sex will be transfixed!"

After the critical success of her first books, *To Bedlam and Part Way Back* and *All My Pretty Ones,* Sexton was frequently criticized for the narrow range and intensity of her preoccupations: always the self, the self as victim, the self as Narcissus, the self as destructive unappeasable bully, more than half in love with sickness and madness and her own "violent heart." Yet *Live or Die* and *Love Poems* attempt a celebration of sorts, however unconvincing it might strike the reader, and in the best poems of these volumes the haranguing voice is exactly right, the ironic, deft, bemused touch never overdone: despite her grim subject matter Sexton has always been a genuinely funny writer when it is her intention to be so. More often the tone is frank, even childlike; the ubiquitous *I* that is sounded throughout all the volumes makes its solemn pronouncements, its vows—"In celebration of the woman I am/and of the soul of the woman I am/and of the central creature and its delight/I sing for you. I dare to live."

Love Poems contains many small measured successes. The poet knows herself "unbalanced" but it is, here, not an issue; she is far more concerned with the bewildering experience of an adulterous love that has had the power to transform her, yet has not the "power" to last. In "For My Lover, Returning to His Wife," language is curt, hard, dry, even sardonic; if there is anger it has been rigorously pared away and the tone now is elegiac. The "victorious" wife is the presence that endures. She is *all there,* while the poet, the mistress, has begun to fade. The wife is "Fireworks in the dull middle of February/and as real as a cast-iron pot." And:

> . . . She is all harmony.
> She sees to oars and oarlocks for the dinghy,
> has placed the wild flowers at the window at breakfast,
> sat by the potter's wheel at midday,
> set forth three children under the moon,
> three cherubs drawn by Michelangelo . . .

"As for me, I am a watercolor," Sexton says. "I wash off." Is she bitter, is she angry, is she merely disappointed? One cannot really judge. One senses her masochistic preoccupation with her own hurt, which blocks a more realistic assessment of the situation; one can see, in a way, through her words to a shadowy guilty self-absorbed lover, whose behavior in the affair is questionable. Her lover has returned to his wife: very well, Sexton seems to think, it is somehow *her* fault, or it is a consequence of the wife's superiority. She does not seem to consider the possibility that the man who has been the object of her excited, almost delirious passion was never, perhaps, equal to her emotion; nor does she consider—but this, too, is an element in her victim's strategy—that the man might be simply shallow, deceitful, childish, a liar. A victim of love customarily looks to himself or herself for all explanations; it is a form of colossal egotism, but a curiously innocent kind. That her former lover deceived his wife and eventually deceived her—that he is, in short, a liar—did not seem to occur to Sexton, and consequently did not draw forth poems of anger and accusation and disgust that might have more satisfactorily rounded off the experience of *Love Poems*.

The volume is prefaced by a quotation from Yeats which is not, I think, altogether appropriate, but it suggests the thematic concerns Sexton believed she had as she organized the book. One should say to himself, according to Yeats:

> I have lived many lives. I have been a slave and
> a prince. Many a beloved has sat upon my knees
> and I have sat upon the knees of many a beloved.
> Everything that has been shall be again.

(That Yeats was an influence of a sort on Sexton is clear from several of the poems, and one in particular, "Just Once," which echoes Yeats's famous "Vacillation" in which the poet, past his fiftieth birthday, suddenly experiences a mystical sense of harmony in a crowded London street. For twenty minutes, Yeats says, it seemed to him that his body "blazed" and "that I was blessèd and could bless." Sexton's poem is more complex, and, sadly, less convincing, except for its predictable conclusion:

> Just once I knew what life was for.
> In Boston, quite suddenly, I understood;
> walked there along the Charles River . . .
> . . . .
> counted the stars, my little campaigners,
> my scar daisies, and knew that I walked my love
> on the night green side of it and cried
> my heart to the eastbound cars and cried
> my heart to the westbound cars and took
> my truth across a small humped bridge
> and hurried my truth, the charm of it, home
> and hoarded these constants into morning
> only to find them gone.)

Elsewhere, there are echoes of Elizabeth Bishop and Whitman, whose deleterious influence on certain strains of American poetry still continues ("In Celebration of My Uterus" with its long catalog of women imagined by Sexton, implausibly joining in a continent-wide hymn to female sexuality and fertility—

> one is in a shoe factory cursing the machine,
> one is at the aquarium tending a seal,
> one is dull at the wheel of her Ford,
> one is at the toll gate collecting,
> one is tying the cord of a calf in Arizona,
> one is straddling a cello in Russia,
> . . . and one is
> anywhere and some are everywhere and all
> seem to be singing, although some can not
> sing a note.)

The majority of the poems, however, attempt a bitterly reflective acerbity reminiscent of Sylvia Plath in *Ariel*. At times the pulse beat of Plath's discordant music is uncanny—one hears it without consciously recognizing it, and one cannot help but wonder if Sexton was altogether conscious of the influence herself. Perhaps she would have excised it had she known. "The room stinks of urine./Only the two-headed baby/is antiseptic in her crib" (from "Eighteen Days Without You"). In the disjointed "Loving the Killer" the poet cries, "Oh my Nazi,/with your S.S. sky-blue eye—/I am no different from Emily Goering." (Elsewhere there is a helpless acquiescence to a lover with a "Nazi hook.") Perhaps most direct is Sexton's statement in "Barefoot": "The surf's a narcotic, calling out,/*I am, I am, I am*/all night long." (Compare with Plath's ". . . his blood beating the old tattoo/I am, I am, I am" from "Suicide Off Egg Rock.") "The trouble was not/in the kitchen or the tulips/but only in my head, my head," Sexton says in "The Touch," alluding to Plath's "Tulips"; but her control of her material is almost always looser than Plath's, and when she is not fuzzily "surreal" (she saw Surrealism as being merely "unconscious") she makes the mistake of being too explicit, too summary. And she has fallen into the habit—a lamentable one in Plath as well—of repeating words to fill out lines. Sometimes the repetition is mechanical, at other times it seems faintly desperate, as in "The Touch"; and it is difficult to know what to make of playful apostrophes like "Oh my love, oh my louse" from the long sequence that ends the book, "Eighteen Days Without You."

But the poems are ultimately her own. The echoes persist, but the vehemence, the decision for life, the prankish multiplication of details are solidly Sexton, as well as the conviction (almost too dogmatically sounded) that love has the miraculous power to transform the personality. Or should. Or did, once. When the memory of the love affair is least burdensome it is most effective. Mistress and lover are conspirators, rather like children. Of course they are sometimes—perhaps often—drunk ("No whatever it was we had,/no sky, no month—just booze"), but their most delightful moments are characterized by a marvelous playfulness that translates itself into some of Sexton's best poetry. It is appropriate that the volume ends with the mistress saying to her lover, "Catch me. I'm your disease," and with the imperatives of "December 18th"—

> Swift boomerang, come get!
> I am delicate. You've been gone.
> The losing has hurt me some, yet
> I must bend for you . . .
>
> . . . .
> Look, lout! Say yes!
> Draw me like a child. I shall need
> merely two round eyes and a small kiss.
> A small o. Two earrings would be nice. Then proceed
> to the shoulder. You may pause at this.
>
> . . . .
> Draw me good, draw me warm.
> Bring me your raw-boned wrist and your
> strange, Mr. Bind, strange stubborn horn.
> Darling, bring with this an hour of undulations, for
> this is the music for which I was born.

Lock in! Be alert, my acrobat
and I will be soft wood and you the nail
and we will make fiery ovens for Jack Sprat
and you will hurl yourself into my tiny jail
and we will take a supper together and that
will be that.

In a characteristically frank memoir of her friend Sylvia Plath, "The Barfly Ought to Sing," published in *Triquarterly* (7, 1970), Anne Sexton made the claim that suicides are special people. "We talked death," she said, "and that was life for us." Unnerving, to imagine these two young and gifted and very attractive women poets exchanging—not news of their poetry, or advice, or even gossip—but details of their suicide attempts! And after Plath's successful attempt some years later, Anne Sexton wrote a poem that belongs with the most despairing and yet the most intelligent and convincing work of what is loosely called the "confessional mode." This poem is "Wanting to Die" and it is included in *Live or Die,* Sexton's third volume. Since her death we may come to think of it as her central poem, the calm, dispassionate, and coolly crafted statement that makes critics' charges of hysteria quite irrelevant:

Since you ask, most days I cannot remember.
I walk in my clothing, unmarked by that voyage.
Then the almost unnameable lust returns.

Even when I have nothing against life.
I know well the grass blades you mention,
the furniture you have placed under the sun.

But suicides have a special language.
Like carpenters they want to know *which tools*.
They never ask *why build*.

Ironically, the thirty-nine poems of Sexton's posthumous volume, *The Awful Rowing Toward God,* do set out reasons, explanations, and occasionally rueful apologies for her emotional predicament; like some of the stronger poems of *The Book of Folly* of 1972, these poems attempt not simply the poetic expression of emotion—that "unstoppered fullness" Robert Lowell praised—but intelligent and sometimes highly critical analysis of the suicidal impulse. In fact, we are mercifully not told *which tools* so much as instructed in the much more valuable *why build*. *The Awful Rowing Toward God* contains poems of superb, unforgettable power, but it would be disingenuous of any reviewer to suppose that the book will be bought and eagerly read for the excellence of its craft. (Many contemporary poets are fine craftsmen, in fact; never have so many people been capable of writing so well, and with so little possibility of being justly recognized.) The book will probably be bought because it is the posthumous volume Anne Sexton had planned and because it describes, with more candor and wit and warmth than Sylvia Plath allowed herself, the stages of the "rowing" toward what Sexton calls "God."

The volume begins with a poem called "Rowing" and ends with "The Rowing Endeth" and the "untamable, eternal, gut driven *ha-ha*" that is the triumph of the union of God and man. Between are poems of sorrow, poems of anger, poems of befuddlement and terror and love, and while some are almost too painful to read ("The Sickness Unto Death," "The Big Heart"), many are as slangy and direct as those "Eighteen Days Without You" that conclude the volume *Love Poems*. In "The Play," for instance, the poet describes herself as the only actor in the play that is her life; she knows her concerns are dismayingly solipsistic, she knows the speeches she gives are "all soliloquies" and that the audience will boo her:

> Despite that I go on to the last lines:
> To be without God is to be a snake
> who wants to swallow an elephant.
> The curtain falls.
> The audience rushes out.
> It was a bad performance.
> That's because I'm the only actor
> and there are few humans whose lives
> will make an interesting play.
> Don't you agree?

There are poets who seem to choose their surreal images with fastidious care, as if seeking physical images to describe what are primarily intellectual or even ideological beliefs; Anne Sexton, however, gives the impression of selecting from a great flood of dreamlike or nightmarish images precisely those which communicate most directly to the reader (and to the poet herself). Her painful honesty is well known. What her unsympathetic critics have charged her with— an overvaluing of her private sorrows to the exclusion of the rest of the world—seems to have been felt by Sexton herself. This sort of knowledge, however, rarely brings with it the ability to *change*. The hearty optimism of a certain kind of American temperament—these days, most obviously illustrated in the plethora of "easy" psychotherapies—is absolutely balked by the fact that some people are unchangeable despite their own deepest wishes; optimists either turn aside from the problem of "evil" (or unhealth), or deny strenuously that it is really a problem. The death-driven personality, whether fated to murder others or itself, is only "neurotic" and can be made more "healthy" by being subjected to the right treatment. Anne Sexton, then, can be dismissed as "sick" and her poetry dismissed as the outpouring of a pathological imagination, unless one is willing to make the risky claim, which will not be a popular one, that poets like Sexton, Plath, and John Berryman have dealt in excruciating detail with collective (and not merely individual) neuroses of our time.

It is probable that a serious artist exercises relatively little control over the choice of subjects of his or her art. The more fortunate artist is simply one who, for reasons not known, identifies powerfully with a unit larger than the self: Faulkner with his "postage stamp" of earth, Shakespeare with the glorious, astounding variety of human personality, Dostoyevsky with all of Russia. Such artists surely dramatize their own emotions, but they give life to the world outside the self by means of these emotions, and in so doing often draw up into consciousness aspects of the collective human self that would otherwise not be tapped. If this sounds like a mysterious process, it must be admitted that it is mysterious: but most artists understand it intuitively. Anne Sexton yearned for that larger experience, that rush of near-divine certainty that the self *is* immortal; she knew it existed but she could not reach it. "The place I live in/is a kind of maze/and I keep seeking/the exit or the home" ("The Children"). Trapped within her specific, private self, she seems to have despaired of any remedy short of actual death—

> . . . I have a body
> and I cannot escape from it.
> I would like to fly out of my head,
> but that is out of the question.
> It is written on the tablet of destiny
> that I am stuck here in this human form.
> That being the case
> I would like to call attention to my problem.
> —"The Poet of Ignorance"

> Only my books anoint me,
> and a few friends,
> those who reach into my veins.
> Maybe I am becoming a hermit,
> opening the door for only
> a few special animals?
> Maybe my skull is too crowded
> and it has no opening through which
> to feed it soup?
> Maybe I have plugged up my sockets
> To keep the gods in?
> —"The Witch's Life"

It is a dismaying journal, not always poetry, though always hopeful of being "poetic." Critical assessment seems somehow beside the point; surely Sexton knew that these poems were not good, that they rambled, faltered, shouted where once they might have whispered, were boozily explicit where once, in the early volumes at least, they would have been enigmatic. "Frenzy" is aptly titled, and one can picture the poet in a frenzy dashing it off—

> I am not lazy.
> I am on the amphetamine of the soul.

I am, each day,
typing out the God
my typewriter believes in.
Very quick. Very intense,
like a wolf at a live heart.

The lover, the faceless giver-of-live, is gone. Even the fairy-tale parents—the evil mother, the inexplicable father—are gone. In their place is Sexton's "God," a child's desperate fantasy, a violent projection that is both stern father and cruel lover, as well as the "body of fate" that cannot be assimilated. Suicides are indeed special people, one senses from reading Sexton, and from reading Plath and Berryman as well: they are children, they have always been children, and no matter how brilliant their minds, they are under the spell, always, of emotions they cannot guess at, and certainly cannot control. As precocious children they delight and terrify us for they strike that chord, in us, which is infantile, and which is certainly *there;* but they go on too long, their self-absorption is finally tedious, the bell jar of their preoccupations will suffocate us—as it did them. Suicide in literature is frequently cleansing: one might speculate that all works of tragedy deal with "suicide" of a kind, as impractical, unworkable, outgrown, inadequate, myopic ideas or states of mind are tested and found lacking. Oedipus's impetuosity brings about his defeat, not his buried "sin"; Lear is frankly silly and unforgivably selfish; Hippolytus's "chastity" is a prig's satisfaction at having no desire. Distance is all: the creator is not absorbed in his subject, though he may give voice to it from the inside. He is dispassionate, contemplative, removed—by the very act of writing he should be removed from the heat, the "frenzy," of inspiration. One knows perfectly well that Dostoyevsky *is* Stavrogin, though he should like to be Bishop Tikhon or Father Zossima; but one knows also that the laborious creation of *The Possessed* and *The Brothers Karamazov* has forced the author into a position of detachment that would have been impossible had the formidable, rather terrifying challenge not been met.

Sexton, of course, could not meet this challenge, which is aesthetic and philosophical as well as—perhaps more important, in fact—psychological. She did not work to imagine a structure that would contain her own small desprairing voice amid many other voices; she did not commit herself to the *labor* of such a creation. For it is a labor. It can be dismayingly difficult: one can be tempted at any point to turn back, to content oneself with the merely personal, the merely local and emotional. "Why not say what happened?" Lowell asks rhetorically, in *Day by Day,* and in general he has been applauded for acquiescing to what, in my opinion, is an imaginative and esthetic impotence: his demon, rather like Sexton's, was not inadequacy in his art, but a strange pride in what might be called the artlessness of the life, the old naturalistic fallacy. (Why invert? Why invert content, or even structures? Simply say what happened.)

The fallacy of such an aesthetic is that one cannot always *know* what has happened. One knows emotions, moods, subjective responses, but rarely their causes; the world becomes smaller and smaller as "external" events are greedily assimilated into a life's scenario. Everything is material for poetry precisely because nothing is given a reality of its own, an integrity—or even an existence—apart from the poet's imagination. In Sexton the experience of "God" is simply another experience of terrible, and terrifying, dependency. The self is small, ravenous for certainty, a "God-monger" that seeks an authority, however improbable, however cruel, that might help to explain the self's predicament. There are moments of contentment, even of joy, in this posthumous volume, poems like "Welcome Morning" and "What the Bird with the Human Head Said" ("Abundance is scooped from abundance,/yet abundance remains"), yet more frequently the tone is breezily fatalistic. Sexton's God is masculine: and being masculine he is inevitably outside her—in fact far away, inaccessible in this life. *God* is simply fate, imagined as an agent that might account for the poet's condition. When she rows, finally, to the Island of God, which is to say to her own death, the two of them play cards and He wins "because He holds five aces" ("The Rowing Endeth"). Sexton does not regret His victory, however—

He starts to laugh,
the laughter rolling like a hoop out of His mouth
and into mine,
and such laughter that He doubles right over me
laughing a Rejoice-Chorus at our two triumphs.
Then I laugh, the fishy dock laughs,
the sea laughs. The Island laughs.
The Absurd laughs.

There is no longer any attempt, we see, at translating emotion into coherent poetic "image." The chilling *ha-ha* of Sexton's last poem is not, as she thought, blissful and all-forgiving: it is a deliberate betrayal of the art set forth so rigorously, and with such memorable power, in the early books. The almost unnameable lust becomes, finally, a lust to destroy poetry itself.

SELF-PORTRAIT IN LETTERS

"A woman who writes feels too much,/those trances and portents!" Anne Sexton exclaimed in a poem titled "The Black Art" (in *All My Pretty Ones,* 1961). No one who has read Sexton's poetry can doubt that she felt "too much" or at any rate excessively; what comes as a surprise is the sheer quantity of writing she did. Quite apart from the nine books of poems she completed, and the play *Mercy Street* which was never published during her lifetime, Anne Sexton wrote lengthy letters nearly every day, complete with carbon copies. At the time of her death in October 1974, she left behind some 50,000 pieces of paper and an enormous collection of memorabilia: boxes of items that constitute, according to the editors of this book, a documentary of her life.

Linda Gray Sexton, Anne's elder daughter, and Lois Ames (a professor of Social Welfare at Northeastern University who is writing the authorized biographies of both Sylvia Plath and Anne Sexton) have put together what will strike some readers as a fascinating book, and others as a possibly premature one. The difficulties the editors faced must have been prodigious. For not only were they confronted with a massive, even dispiriting quantity of letters of uneven worth; they were also confronted with the very real problem of sifting through these letters with an eye for what might be construed as an invasion of privacy by Anne's friends, acquaintances, and relatives. (And enemies. Anne's *bête noir* seems to have been James Dickey, who not only savagely reviewed one of her books for the *New York Times* but seems to have been quite ardent in his pursuit of her for a year or two afterward.)

This autobiography in letters is an extraordinarily difficult book to read, and a still more difficult book to review. How, after all, does one presume to review a life . . . ? How can one assess a "self-portrait in letters" in meaningful critical terms? Readers who admire Sexton's poetry will find much to admire in the letters, but they will also find much to cause grief; and they will surely wish that Linda Sexton and Lois Ames had edited the collection even more judiciously. (For there are innumerable letters that must have been written while Sexton was heavily drugged, or in a drunken stupor, and one very much doubts that she would have wished them printed.) Readers who have not admired the poetry will find the letters nearly impossible to read, for they not only dwell upon the poet's relationship to her art in great detail but they set forth, without the often complex strategies of that art, the same feelings—the same raw, ungovernable, inchoate emotions—that fueled it.

"Madness," Sexton said to a disturbed fan who had written to her, in 1965, "is a waste of time. It creates nothing. . . . Nothing grows from it and you, meanwhile, only grow into it like a snail." It is clear from her letters that Anne Sexton resisted her own madness, at least most of the time. She seems always to have dramatized herself— even as a child she had a wild, uncontrollable craving to be noticed— but at the same time a sterner, harsher wisdom cautioned her against succumbing to the self-consuming "energies" of the demonic. What is extraordinary about the letters, and in fact one of their redeeming features, is the tone the poet takes when she addresses correspondents who are recognizably sick. In writing to friends and acquaintances like W. D. Snodgrass, Maxine Kumin, Lois Ames, and others who are engrossed in their own work and lives, Anne is at times astonishingly effusive; her letters to Snodgrass—"Snodsy"—are almost hysterical, and must have caused him some exasperation and pain. But letters written to emotionally unbalanced acquaintances are remarkably sober. It is as if the carapace of gay, insouciant energy were dropped, and in its place Anne Sexton speaks with the restraint of one of her own psychiatrists. To a monk who seems to have fallen in love with her, or who has at any rate suffered a violent projection of his fantasies onto her, Sexton is quick to point out that the letters she has written to him are not, in an important way, "real." In letters it is possible, she says, to be loving and lovable, more possible to reach out and to take in, "and no one really need live up to them." Having excited in the man emotions she had not anticipated, she draws back, prudently: "Oh dear God. You must listen to me, for I feel I have somehow deceived you into thinking this is really a human relationship. It is a letter relationship. . . ."

Elsewhere, in writing to one "Philip Barlow," a university professor who seems, like the young monk, to have fallen in love with an image of her, Anne is equally sober. "Yes we love each other—but it's a mirror—of sorts—it's the male of the female and the female of the male. In other words, you're me. Also I'm you. . . . This way leads us both into madness." Such a love is "sick" and a lover locked into such an obsession needs professional help. And in writing to the innumerable would-be poets who wanted her advice, and her friendship, Sexton is helpful indeed. She cautions them to discipline themselves; to labor at their craft without impatience; and to study Rilke's *Letters to a Young Poet,* one of her favorite books.

Among the many recipients of Anne's letters over the years are Maxine Kumin (of whom she says in a letter to someone else, "Thank God for Maxine. She is close by always and knows me. No one else who is within literal reach allows me to be real or to think"); Tillie Olsen, whose "Tell Me a Riddle" impressed her greatly; "Dr. Anne Clarke," a California psychiatrist with whom she seems to have identified strongly, and to whom she speaks most openly about her psychological distress and her obsession with suicide (". . . You have a certain power . . . power over what? well, life for instance . . . and death too. I guess I see [suicide] as a way of cheating death"); W. D. Snodgrass, to whom she sent many of her poems after having been his student at the Antioch Writers' Summer Conference in 1958, and whose *Heart's Needle* greatly inspired her; Robert Lowell, whose student she was in a writing seminar at Boston University, and about whom she says in a letter to Snodgrass ("I guess I forgive him for not liking me . . . because he has such a soft dangerous voice. . . . He is a good man; I forgive him for his sicknesses whatever they are. I think I will have to god *[sic]* him again; gods are so necessary and splendid and distant"); Nolan Miller of the *Antioch Review,* which was the first quality magazine to publish her poetry; Carolyn Kizer, then of *Poetry Northwest,* who took the time to criticize Anne's submissions in detail; John Holmes, whom she met in a Boston poetry workshop; Hollis Summers, whom she met at Antioch and who seems to have intrigued her because he did not succumb to her need for intimacy ("I, frankly, do not mind you not being in love with me. Really. No need to be in love with me. But must you be frightened of me?"); Frederick Morgan of *The Hudson Review,* whose early encouragement helped her greatly; Louis Simpson, whose work she admired ("I would write just like you if I could"); Philip Rahv of *The Partisan Review,* who published some of her poems; Anthony Hecht, a close friend in the early 1960s who seems also to have drawn back from Anne's intensity ("I think that I'm cross with you. . . . When you say that I am giving vent to a wild, romantic fantasy of a rather suspect kind. . . . What I meant very simply is that I love you . . . but that I'm not *in love* with you. . . . I don't dislike you for coming back with your feelings on the subject but I am very cross with you for not allowing me some room for a very female emotion that wasn't meant to bother you or tempt you . . ."); Galway Kinnell; Jon Stallworthy; Charles Newman, who invited her to participate in a special issue of *TriQuarterly* devoted to the work of Sylvia Plath; James Dickey ("I do not want or look for a *mad passionate* affair. . . . I would run to the end of town to avoid it. . . . please believe me, I do not want a lover.

. . . I want a friend. . . . I cannot promise that I am geared to your kind of self," and, later: "My instincts keep going two ways about you. One says it's O.K., the other says be careful. After I met you, in New York State, I heard nothing but gossip about you. Things rather nasty . . ."); Robert Bly; Ted Hughes; C. K. Williams, one of her favorite new poets, whose first book she encouraged Houghton Mifflin to publish in 1968; George Starbuck; and Stanley Kunitz, to whom she sent *Transformations* in manuscript, in 1970, and whose praise for the experimental work was highly supportive.

The most spontaneous letters are those to her daughters Linda and Joyce (the last letter she wrote before her suicide was a tender note to Linda), and to her husband "Kayo" (Alfred Sexton II). Their marriage seems to have been, for the most part, a good one, yet Anne insisted upon a divorce in 1973, after twenty-four years of marriage; and by October 1974 she was dead.

"I wonder if the artist ever lives his life—he is so busy recreating it," Sexton said in a letter of 1972. "Only as I write do I realize myself. I don't know what that does to 'life.' " One of the difficulties with such a position—whether it is philosophical, or emotional—is that the poet's distrust of his own most powerful instincts works against the highest realization of those instincts. If one believes that artistic re-creation of one's life is in some way antithetical to life, or even peripheral to it, art itself will come to seem destructive. "Yet," says Anne Sexton in one of her last poems, "I am in love with words." Her combative relationship with herself, the near-ceaseless warring between a violent will to live and an even more violent and insidious will to die, allowed her, for a brief, intense period of time, the transcendence of genuine art. The poetry did not cause her death, but postponed it: in that sense Anne Sexton the poet was a triumph, a triumphant event in our literature. Though her later books—*The Death Notebooks, The Awful Rowing Toward God, The Book of Folly*—display a deterioration of vision and control, partly as a consequence of her drug-and-alcohol addiction, there is achievement of the highest quality in *To Bedlam and Part Way Back, All My Pretty Ones,* and *Live Or Die.*

Anne Sexton's letters are, as she knew, too breezy, too disjointed and emotional to compete with her art, and the question of whether she would have wished her letters published will probably be raised. (She *did* keep carbon copies, after all, and evidently, near the end of her life, willed to "re-create" herself through these letters—that is, explain herself, defend herself, attempt to enlist others in her feuds with relatives, friends, and professional acquaintances. One wonders, in fact, whether the poet was not consciously creating an artificial persona.) It might also be pointed out that, in order to avoid injuring people, and in order to avoid lawsuits, the editors have been forced to censor many letters, and to leave out others altogether. Consequently we learn very little about the reasons behind Anne Sexton's sudden desire for a divorce, which her husband contested; we learn nothing at all about a "disastrous love affair" she evidently had during the last year of her life. Though *Anne Sexton: A Self-Portrait in Letters* is a remarkably rich and detailed book, it does read like a novel whose final pages have been ripped out. What might the editors have done? Delay publication for many years? (A tradition that seems to be fast fading in our culture.) That the letters are, in this version, incomplete and possibly misleading cannot be helped; yet to delay publication until all the letters could be published would perhaps be quixotic, since interest in Sexton is high at the present time, and is apt to diminish as the years pass.

In the end one feels that Sexton would be pleased with this book, for it is, after all, *hers*. Her voice is there, on every page; her presence is mesmerizing, indefatigable. And she came not to care very much whether her vision was "artful" or not: she was a witness of her own life, her own destruction, and perhaps there is a communicable wisdom in the very experience of breakdown, emotional and esthetic both. How else might we interpret such poems as "The Play," in *The Awful Rowing Toward God*—

> Suddenly I stop running.
> (This moves the plot along a bit.)
> I give speeches, hundreds,
> all prayers, all soliloquies.
> I say absurd things like:
> eggs must not quarrel with stones

or keep your broken arm inside your sleeve
or I am standing upright
but my shadow is crooked.
And such and such.
Many boos. Many boos.

If there is a kind of courage in the final, most brutal exposure of the self, the artist's presentation of himself without the qualifying guise of his art, then Anne Sexton was a highly courageous woman. One cannot read her poetry, or her letters, without being both deeply disturbed and moved.

Sacred and Profane
Iris Murdoch

Though Iris Murdoch has defined the highest art as that which reveals and honors the minute, "random" detail of the world, and reveals it together with a sense of its integrity, its unity and form, her own ambitious, disturbing, and eerily eccentric novels are stichomythic structures in which ideas, not things, and certainly not human beings, flourish. In the beginning *is* the Word.

There are many novels—*The Sea, The Sea* is the nineteenth—and many characters, and many wildly, at times frantically, inventive plots. There are perhaps hundreds of interiors, meticulously described; and hundreds of costumes; and a small galaxy of observations about the quality of the air, the sun's setting or the sun's rising, the condition of London in the summer, or in the fall, or in the rainy winter, or the bright misleading spring. There are innumerable

Iris Murdoch, *The Sea, The Sea* (New York: Viking Press, 1978).

"loves"—usually one dominant love to a novel, and satellite, subplot loves that mock or confirm the central love-obsession. There are characters who are "enchanters" (often self-deceived) and characters who are "enchanted," often disastrously. There are convoluted plots reminiscent of the worst of Elizabethan and Jacobean plays, and the most cheerfully muddled of Restoration comedies, in which the author operates, at times almost visibly, as a puppet-mistress alternately contemptuous of and moved by her characters' fates. There are defiantly tidy endings, as in *The Time of the Angels* and *The Italian Girl,* inferior works; and unresolved, troubling, provocative endings, as in *A Word Child, The Sacred and Profane Love Machine, Henry and Cato,* and *The Sea, The Sea*—loose, freer, more ribald, even rather buffoonish works that, while never experimental in a literary sense, are nevertheless not contained by the rigid theatrical structures and "unexpected" disclosures of a more conventional novelistic vision. There is a dizzying profusion, then, of characters, incidents, settings, "endings," so much so that even admirers of Murdoch's fiction often complain that they cannot remember a novel only a few days after having read it. (Indeed, the protagonist of *The Sea, The Sea,* a retired playwright and director who has achieved great fame in England, but who sees himself, correctly, as an egotist and a rapacious magician, is charged by a former admirer with having created nothing genuine, nothing of permanent value: Charles Arrowby is a master of dazzling ephemera, nothing more, and now that his power is fading he will soon be forgotten. Like Hilary Burde of *A Word Child* and, to some extent, the overly prolific, death-haunted novelist Montague Small of *The Sacred and Profane Love Machine,* Arrowby must be speaking of matters with which Murdoch is personally concerned.)

Despite this multiplicity, this richness, however, the novels are not really difficult, so long as one reads them as structures in which ideas compete, as in a debate, or, when they are most successful, as in Greek tragedy, in which near-symmetrical, balanced forces war with one another. The question is never, Which vision of the cosmos is most reasonable, most deserving of victory? but, rather, Which vision of the cosmos coincides with that of the gods? (By *gods* is meant simply the objective, impersonal, ineluctable pattern of the universe, in which human subjectivity, and all the wishful stains of self, are dissolved.)

Self as blinding, crippling, paralyzing, ludicrous: this seems to be Murdoch's position. She has said that the greatest art, like that of Shakespeare, is impersonal; it contemplates and delineates nature with a "clear eye," untainted by fantasy. Why subjectivity and even the private self's fantasies should be so abhorred by Murdoch, and denied a place, a weight, in the cosmos (for surely it is as "real" as the material world, or the collective fantasies we call culture), is never altogether clear in her philosophical writings or in her fiction. In an elegiac poem, "Agamemnon Class 1939"* Murdoch states in serene, stately language, addressed to a dead classmate, that the "demons" that traveled with them in their youth were still, in 1939, "smiling in their sleep." Terrible violence will come in the *Agamemnon,* terrible violence will come in the world:

> No one can rebuild that town
> And the soldier who came home
> Has entered the machine of a continued doom.
> Only the sky and the sea
> Are unpolluted and old
> And godless with innocence.
> And twilight comes to the chasm
> And to the sea's expanse
> And the terrible bright Greek air fades away.

Murdoch's implicit philosophical position is austere, classical, rigorously unromantic, and pessimistic. Not that pessimism precludes comedy: on the contrary, it is probably the basis of the comic spirit.

Life after all is comic, not tragic, in Murdoch's cosmology. It is comic *because* it is not tragic—merely terrible. (As Charles Arrowby says at the start of *The Sea, The Sea,* ironically, since he will soon be

Boston University Journal, Vol. XXV, no. 2, p. 57.

caught up in an absurd delusion of his own: "The theatre apes the profound truth that we are extended beings who yet can only exist in the present. It is a factitious present because it lacks the free aura of personal reflection and contains its own secret limits and conclusions.") Nothing is so fascinating, so enigmatic, as the nature of the Good, and of Love, and Freedom: yet nothing is so elusive, and brings us to such muddles (to use a word that Murdoch employs often). There are even amusing Murdoch characters who realize that they are doomed to happiness and to the mediocrity that seems to imply, since the circumstances of their lives prevent them from continuing the quest for the nature of truth (Henry Marshalson, Bruno's son Miles). But suffering itself, in the context of pitiless self-examination, can masquerade as purification, and we are back where we've begun—no more enlightened than before. There is a marvelous moment at the end of Murdoch's essay "On 'God' and 'Good' " (in *The Sovereignty of Good*, 1970) when the author, after many pages of abstract, rather tortuous theorizing, changes tone suddenly: "At this point someone might say, all this is very well, the only difficulty is that none of it is true." And, consequently: "Perhaps indeed all is vanity, *all* is vanity, and there is no respectable intellectual way of protecting people from despair."

There is something noble about a philosopher's quixotic assumption that he or she is the person to protect others from despair; or, indeed, that others require protection from despair. But Murdoch's sense of her mission *is* noble, and in an era when some of our most articulate spokesmen routinely denigrate their own efforts it is good to be told, I think plausibly, that literature provides a very real education in how to picture and comprehend the human situation, and that for both the collective and individual *salvation* of the race, art is more important than anything else, and literature most important of all. (See *The Sovereignty of Good*.)

To a Platonist ideas are real. Iris Murdoch is, perhaps, not a Platonist—not quite. And yet in her novels ideas are far more "real" than they are in other contemporary novels, and there are not very many of them, and they are clearly, almost too clearly, set forth. The basic idea seems to be that centuries of humanism have nourished an unrealistic conception of the powers of the will: we have gradually lost the vision of a reality separate from ourselves, and we have no adequate conception of original sin. Twentieth-century obsessions with the authority of the individual, the "existential" significance of subjectivity, are surely misguided, for the individual cannot be (as he thinks himself, proudly) a detached observer, free to invent or reimagine his life. *The Time of the Angels* is one of Murdoch's least plausible novels, but its mock existential Death-of-God concerns are illuminating. If there is no God, as Dostoyevsky said, is it possible that everything is permitted?—nothing is *not* permitted? Carl Fisher, the suicidal fallen priest of *The Time of the Angels*, once began a sermon by saying, "And what if I tell you there is no God?" and spends most of his time, and the reader's, in a quite literal fog, toying with ideas of freedom, nihilism, crime, and death. He is Murdoch's quite serious embodiment of the necessary consequences of fashionable godless Existentialism, and there are times when his thoughts, and even his language, echo those of Dostoyevsky's formidable Svidrigalov. The "death" of God has set His thoughts (or angels) free, and these thoughts are beyond our conception in their power. As Christianity dissolves, might it be that a great curtain will be raised at last, and, if so, what might be revealed behind . . . ? Carl Fisher commits suicide because his "black philosophy" is simply lifeless, and the ordinary world resumes its power: the London fog lifts. In *The Nice and the Good* it is observed that there are mysterious agencies of the mind, gaseous tentacles that can cause pain and mutilation: the ordinary person is naturally endowed with them, "just as he is endowed with the ghostly power of appearing in other people's dreams." These eidola projected from the mind can become autonomous, wandering freely in search of victims, unless, of course, they are stopped by the sacrificial act of one who is both good and at the same time disinterested. But since our original sin is, quite probably, our infatuation with self, so this expulsion of random, brute evil is extremely difficult: how does one transcend one's own self, without delusion?

In *The Sea, The Sea* Charles Arrowby's escape from London and his attempt to purge himself of egoism by writing his autobiography—near the appropriately named village of Narrowdean—is a gesture that might seem laudable; yet it is fraught with risk, and eventually brings disaster upon himself and others, precisely because it is an artificial, and even subtly satanic, act. For Arrowby cannot help revising his life, even as he recounts it. Murdoch believes that the "inner" world is, in a sense, parasitic upon the "outer" world, and that love, far from being the redemptive, all-consuming force that sentimentalists consider it, is in fact the most dangerous of all delusions. It is bound up helplessly with egoism and personal fantasy, the "tissue of self-aggrandizing and consoling wishes and dreams which prevent one from seeing what there is outside one," and it is, fairly normally, too myopic, possessive, and "mechanical" to aid one in a realistic interpretation of the universe. Mankind is not free. There are few choices, few options, though daydreams and fantasies urge us to believe that there are many, and that the small, distorting window through which we view the world is not a fiction. It has been charged that Murdoch's characters are puppets and that they are jerked about from one improbable crisis to another, and perhaps in response to this Murdoch has had one of her most important spokesmen, Brendan, Cato's mentor in *Henry and Cato,* say that people *are* puppets—puppets in the hands of God. And what is God? "God is unimaginable and incomprehensible and nameless. *Dysphrastos* and *thaumastos.*" Perhaps God is simply another fiction, however, and the various metaphysical substitutes—Reason, Science, History, Society, "Progress"—are false deities. One is left, then, with . . .

One is left with silly inconsequential but deeply absorbing plots. Emotions that feel "genuine" and "existential" enough but are, of course, illusions, sheer phantasmagoria. One is left with other people who are, whether they acknowledge it or not, involved in the same fruitless, albeit highly engrossing, quest. Their "ideas" make war upon one another; their "visions" are always in conflict. Charles Arrowby imagines himself the most rigorous of thinkers, shrewd, analytic, unsparing of self, yet he is seduced by a grotesquely sentimental—and, alas, not always convincing—notion of destiny: he meets the woman who was his first love, more than forty years ago, and, though she is of course much changed, is in fact unattractive and not very bright, and terribly boring, he becomes obsessed with her, imagines that he is madly in love with her, and that it is his duty to rescue her from her dull, routinely unhappy marriage. (A device that Murdoch has used in the past, often more successfully: the imposing of the lover's vision of his love onto a real, unfortunate, rather bewildered victim. So Henry Marshalson of *Henry and Cato,* in a futile attempt to postpone his own ineludible destiny, talks himself into "falling in love" with and "wanting to marry" a very ordinary woman whom he imagined his dead brother loved; so Hilary Burde and Lady Kitty of *A Word Child* enter passionately into a *folie à deux* that is fatal to Lady Kitty and comes near to destroying the self-important, imperious Hilary, the "word child," himself.) *The Sea, The Sea* is intermittently brilliant, given life by those off-hand, gnomic, always provocative remarks—essays in miniature, really— that characterize Murdoch's novels, and give them their intelligence, their gravity, while the machinations of the plot threaten to dissipate all seriousness; but Charles Arrowby's obsessive, fantasizing concern with his old love Hartley, who rejected him at the age of twenty and married someone else, and who has become a comically inappropriate image of Young Love and Lost Innocence, is not made very convincing. Scene follows scene, the movement of Charles's mind is maddeningly sluggish, one comes to feel that Murdoch is not going to *budge,* and that the strategy of a first-person narrator (so effective in *A Word Child*) was simply an error in *The Sea, The Sea.* Curiously, the novel is not very dramatic. There are a few awkward gestures toward gothic melodrama: Charles is terrified when a mirror is broken in his house, and a vase smashed; he believes he has seen a sea-serpent and a dim "ghost"—but the "supernatural" is set aside for hundreds of pages, and some of the acts rather perfunctorily explained, so that Charles can concentrate upon his quixotic, doomed "love" for poor Hartley, the "Bearded Lady." There is a genuine accident—Hartley's adopted son Titus drowns in the sea; there is an attempted murder—Charles himself is pushed into the sea, not by Hartley's jealous husband, as he thinks, but by one of his "admirers" who, he comes to learn, has secretly detested him for years. But much of the novel is static, and Charles becomes unforgivably garrulous. He *is* a vain, self-important fool, yet one resents being trapped inside his consciousness, however authentic it seems. And it is difficult not to think that the novel's conclusion, which involves the "supernatural" powers of Charles's envied cousin James, who has disciplined himself in Buddhist practices, and is evidently capable of committing a painless, bloodless suicide by exerting "just a little pressure of his mind upon his body" so that his consciousness is extinguished forever, is not part of another novel, another extended vision.

There are too many sketchy characters in *The Sea, The Sea,* the "fable" is not adequately linked to the "theme," and Murdoch is coming to depend upon a certain category of personage—Brendan of *Henry and Cato,* Willy Kost of *The Nice and the Good,* Arthur of *A Word Child,* Edgar of *The Sacred and Profane Love Machines,* Max Lejour of *The Unicorn,* Matthew of *An Accidental Man,* Carl Fisher of *The Time of the Angels,* Nigel of *Bruno's Dream,* etc.—far too often, too glibly, in order to make her primary ideas explicit. The employment of highly articulate characters if of course not an inevitable sign of a novel's failure: Dostoyevsky uses such characters frequently, and among them are some of his most brilliant creations (Father Zossima, Porfiry, the dying Stepan Verkhovensky), and nearly all of Lawrence's major figures are used as vehicles, sometimes shamelessly so, for Lawrence's ideas.

But in Murdoch these characters are used repeatedly; they are self-conscious gods-from-the-machine who confront the protagonist with certain gnomic observations that might be applicable to any human dilemma. The wise, gentle Arthur of *A Word Child* says, in defense of Buddhism, which Hilary has attacked, "I don't think we all exist that much. I think we should just be kind to one another. . . . I mean one's mind is just an accidental jumble of stuff. There's nothing behind ordinary life. There isn't anything complete. Life isn't a play. It isn't even a pantomime." But Hilary, who is almost literally an underground man (he loves to ride the Underground beneath the city of London, seeing it as his natural home; the Inner Circle is his favorite) cannot absorb his wisdom. In *The Sacred and Profane Love Machine*, one of Murdoch's most energetically muddled novels, the peculiar Edgar Demarnay tells David, a young victim, that he must forgive and forget those who have injured him: he must not judge. "One mustn't worry too much. All human solutions are temporary. . . . One's ordinary tasks are usually immediate and simple and one's own truth lives in these tasks. Not to deceive oneself, not to protect one's pride with false ideas, never to be pretentious or bogus, always to try to be lucid and quiet. There's a kind of pure speech of the mind which one must try to attain. To attain it is to be in the truth, one's own truth, which needn't mean any big apparatus of belief. And when one is *there* one will be truthful and kind and able to see other people and what they need!"

Murdoch makes an attempt to give such characters weight, to sketch in backgrounds for them—they usually have "tragic" memories—but they remain unconvincing because they are so dangerously close to the authorial voice itself. All *is* illusion—in art, in the pages of a novel; but fictional characters, at least in conventionally imagined novels like Murdoch's, are not supposed to know that they are part of an illusion or that it is, in an ultimate sense, not very significant. These spokesmen strike the reader as unreal because they are no more than ideas, the embodiment of ideas, and constitute, in a sense, the novelist's failure to communicate her theme on a deeper, less self-consciously verbal level; or perhaps it is an impatience with the formality of the novel itself. One has the typically dense Murdochian plot with its cast of highly idiosyncratic characters, and one has a kind of ongoing choral commentary on the plot and characters. When the story, the people, are convincingly imagined—as in *Henry and Cato,* Murdoch's finest novel to date, and surely one of the major achievements in fiction in recent years—one is not distracted by the commentary; when the story and its people are sketchily imagined, too obviously arbitrary and clownish to be worthy of our serious attention, the thematic statements, the Olympian utterances, fail to work entirely. We are told in novel after novel that people are "mechanical," that erotic love is a sort of "machine," that Goodness is "giving up power and acting upon the world negatively," that lusts and attachments compose the ordinary person's god, and that it is only by giving up such illusions that one can achieve freedom, but such remarks are only significant in terms of the specific images, the specific people (or illusions, perhaps) they seek to illuminate. Where ideas float about, inadequately embodied in narrative, they are often fascinating in themselves—and surely Murdoch is one of our most consistently intelligent, and rewarding, writers—but the danger is, of course, that they will come to seem increasingly perfunctory. One does not read *The Brothers Karamazov* to be told that "God is love," though Dostoyevsky might have imagined that that was his primary reason for writing it.

In *The Nice and the Good* a character who wants, like Charles Arrowby, to be *good,* states: ". . . In order to become good it may be necessary to imagine oneself good, and yet such imagining may also be the very thing which renders improvement impossible, either because of surreptitious complacency or because of . . . blasphemous infection . . . when goodness is thought about in the wrong way." A succinct commentary on the would-be Prospero, Charles, who resorts to bullying, trickery, deception, and finally kidnapping in order to make his "love" realize that the two of them are bound together in an eternal bond. By his meddling Charles awakens a demon of some sort, sets into action the "deadly machine" that will lead to the drowning of Hartley's son, and brings about his loss of Hartley; but it is one of the more ingenious elements of the novel that, like the insufferable "accidental man" of the novel of that title, Charles Arrowby is himself unharmed. He hurts others, experiences pain and suffering, imagines himself "blessed," but returns to busy, superficial London and his old life; for life, Charles says, unlike art, "has an irritating way of bumping and limping on, undoing conversions, casting doubt on solutions, and generally illustrating the impossibility of living happily or virtuously ever after." At the novel's very end Charles has made a luncheon date with a seventeen-year-old virgin who wants to have his son; she is obviously deranged, but charmingly so, like the exasperating Kiki St. Loy of *The Sacred and Profane Love Machine*. Charles notes that a Buddhist "demon casket" belonging to his late cousin James has fallen over, and its lid come off, and in all innocence he inquires: "Upon the demon-ridden pilgrimage of human life, what next I wonder?"

A witty conclusion to an uneven but provocative novel, and one that might appropriately conclude any of Murdoch's works. We are offered unanticipated moments of terrible, even tragic lucidity; we *are* purified by suffering; but our powerful revelations fade, our insights dissolve, and we are back in the world of appearances, of strife and desire and illusion. Given the opportunity to experience freedom we prefer to be, in the end, puppets of God. The work that is central to an understanding of Murdoch's oeuvre is Plato's allegory of the cave: I suggest that all of Murdoch's novels are commentaries on it.

Flannery O'Connor

A SELF-PORTRAIT IN LETTERS

Profundity, Nietzsche said, loves the mask. And so it will be no surprise to admirers of Flannery O'Connor's enigmatic, troubling, and highly idiosyncratic fiction to learn that there were, behind the near-perfect little rituals of violence and redemption she created, not one but several Flannery O'Connors. And how wildly they differed. . . . The experience of reading these collected letters (which are, in fact, rigorously *selected* letters) is a disturbing one: but tonic, provocative, intriguing. For while it cannot be said of Flannery O'Connor's fiction that she revealed herself anywhere within it—her strategy was to submerge herself, to "correct" emotion by means of art—it must be said of the letters that they give life to a wonderfully warm, witty, generous, and complex personality, surely one of the most gifted of contemporary writers. At the same time they reveal a curiously

Flannery O'Connor, *The Habit of Being: Letters, edited and with an Introduction by Sally Fitzgerald* (New York: Farrar, Straus & Giroux, 1979).

girlish, childlike, touchingly timid personality, so conventional that the very idea of allowing James Baldwin to visit her in Milledgeville, Georgia, in 1959 frightened her into saying that she observed the traditions of the society she fed upon (which was, in most respects, defiantly untrue)—and that the meeting, "innocent" elsewhere, would cause her the "greatest trouble and disturbance and disunion" in Georgia. The letters give voice, on one side, to a hilariously witty observer of the grotesque, the vulgar, and the merely silly in this society, and in the rather limited world of the Catholic imagination; and then they reveal a Catholic intellectual so conservative and docile that she will write to a priest-friend for permission to read Gide and Sartre (at that time on the Church's Index of forbidden writers)— and she will remark, to another friend, that the Church is correct in "warning" believers against Teilhard de Chardin since his work is "incomplete and unclear on the subject of grace." Her view of "Cathlicks" was by no means a sentimental one; she knew that, as she said so succinctly, "The silence of the Catholic critic is so often preferable to his attention." (She did indeed endure ignorant misinterpretations of her work.) But then she will piously condemn the film of Tennessee Williams's *Baby Doll* as a "dirty little piece of trash"—without having seen it.

A brief review is not the place to count, even to categorize, aspects of personality: masks, voices, disingenuous roles. But I counted at least five distinctly different Flannery O'Connors here, in these pages, and it struck me as highly interesting that the O'Connor of the fiction is nowhere present. She simply doesn't exist—in the letters. She exists, as she must, only—and supremely—in the fiction. One should not read *The Habit of Being* with the hope of penetrating the "secret" of Flannery O'Connor's art, or even with the hope of learning more about her intentions and habits of composition than is already available in her posthumous collection of essays, *Mystery and Manners*. She wrote slowly, so slowly that it took her the same length of time (seven years) to write the brief, spare *The Violent Bear It Away* that it took Joyce to write *Ulysses*. (And Joyce too suffered ill-health.) Each paragraph, each sentence, each word was written with great deliberation, and rewritten, and rewritten, so that the final product—austere, "comic," allegorical, parable-like—was inevitably somewhat artificial, and inevitably profound. The person, the woman, the gracious, rather shy Southern girl Flannery, certainly could not embody such high seriousness in her being. She says in a letter to Elizabeth Hardwick and Robert Lowell, in 1954: ". . . I don't look very intelligent. I was in Nashville . . . and met a man who looked at me a while and said (of *Wise Blood*), 'That was a profound book. You don't look like you wrote it.' I mustered up my squintiest expression and snarled, 'Well I did,' but at the same time I had to recognize he was right." Apart from such rare remarks she seems not to have been troubled in the slightest by the contradictory, even warring aspects of her personality. If something disturbed her enough it found its way, no doubt, into her art: it did not touch her life. Or so it would seem, judging from the evidence of *The Habit of Being*.

The first letter in the collection was written in 1948, when Flannery was "up north" at Yaddo, the writers' colony in Saratoga Springs. (I am following Sally Fitzgerald in referring to Flannery O'Connor as *Flannery:* the full name seems inappropriately formal.) The last letter, a heartbreaking one, was written just before her death on August 3, 1964, when she knew she was dying (she had already taken the Sacrament of the Sick a month earlier) of complications following an operation for the removal of a tumor. The years between 1948 and 1964 were rich, full ones, despite the fact that Flannery's debilitating condition (lupus) kept her at home, and frequently bedridden, for long periods of time. She was not at all a solitary, reclusive person; she had a wide circle of friends and acquaintances, and clearly loved seeing them, and writing to them often. Among her "literary" and "interleteckchul" friends were Caroline Gordon and Allen Tate; Elizabeth Hardwick and Robert Lowell; Richard Stern; Robie Macauley; Elizabeth Bishop; Granville Hicks; John Hawkes; Walker Percy; J. F. Powers; Marion Montgomery; Robert Giroux (her editor); Andrew Lytle; and of course Sally and Robert Fitzgerald, at whose home in Connecticut she stayed. (She was evidently friendly with James Dickey as well, but for some reason no letters of hers to Dickey are reprinted here.) All the letters are warm, frank, bright, and courteous; only a few exhibit impatience with asinine questions about the deep symbolic meaning of her stories, put to her by "professors of English" and their students, and indefatigable pseudo-Freudians given to hallucinating phallic imagery on every page. (Perhaps Flannery was too kind, and wasted her tragically limited energies . . . ? It is a pity that she felt obliged to reply to people who clearly misunderstood her work, or who took offense at it, as if she felt, despite her confidence in her art, that she must defend it. Her sharpest remark—which is very much justified— is made in response to a "litterary" person's queries about Freudian imagery in *The Violent Bear It Away:* "I'm sorry the book didn't come off for you but I think it is no wonder it didn't since you see everything in terms of sex symbols. . . . My Lord, Billy, recover your simplicity. You ain't in Manhattan. Don't inflict that stuff on the poor students there; they deserve better."

The most unanticipated, and perhaps the most unsettling, of the various Flannerys is the disingenuous hick, the self-conscious, self-mocking bumpkin who emerges in certain letters with great zest. This is the Flannery who never hesitates to make bad jokes and puns, to misspell words in a coyly illiterate way, to tell outrageous tales about Georgia doings; she refers to her *Opus nauseous,* she alludes to the tragedy of *Edipus,* she sprinkles her comments freely with "aint," "it don't," "yestiddy," "naw," "bidnis," "Cathlicks," "pilgrumidge," "litterary." The affectation of a sub-Socratic irony may strike some readers as embarrassing, particularly when it is overdone; and despite Sally Fitzgerald's insistence in her excellent introduction that Flannery loved and respected her mother, Regina, it is difficult to know how to interpret the numerous comic sketches in which Regina appears, often as a good-natured, bumbling idiot. The portrait is funny but cruel. But it *is* funny:

> My mamma and I have interesting literary discussions like the following which took place over some Modern Library books I had just ordered:

SHE: *"Mobby Dick.* I've always heard about that."

ME: *"Mow-by Dick."*

SHE: *"Mow-by Dick. The Idiot.* You would get something called *Idiot.*
       What's it about?"

ME: "An idiot." (From a letter of February 1953)

Regina is getting very literary. "Who is this Kafka?" she says.
"People ask me." A German Jew, I says, I think. He wrote a book
about a man who turns into a roach. "Well, I can't tell people
that," she says. "Who is this Evalin Wow?"

Poor hapless Regina struggles with stray mules and with her hired
help, who are every bit as grotesque as the poor whites in Flannery's
stories; she despairs over her daughter's diction and her evident
disdain for the more explicit Southern graces. She tells Flannery in
exasperation, "You talk just like a nigger and someday you are going
to be away from home and do it and people are going to wonder
WHERE YOU CAME FROM." Certainly Flannery was hiding behind
this mask, and yet one must assume that it *did* express her feelings, for
there is a consistency about her country-cousinish persona that
suggests the shrewd simplicity of a number of her characters. From a
letter to Richard Stern, July 1963:

> What you ought to do is get you a Fulbright to Georgia and quit
> messing around with all those backward places you been at.
> Anyhow, don't pay a bit of attention to the Eyetalian papers. . . .
> All us niggers and white folks over here are just getting along
> grand—at least in Georgia and Mississippi. I hear things are not
> so good in Chicago and Brooklyn but you wouldn't expect them
> to know what to do with theirself there.

Then there is the conservative Catholic, who would seem, in my
imagination at least, to seriously underestimate the artist: as if
Flannery the docile, "good" little girl, schooled by nuns, were
incapable of comprehending the other Flannery's gifts. Again and

again she insists that "I write the way I do because and only because I am a Catholic. I feel that if I were not a Catholic, I would have no reason to write, no reason to see, no reason ever to feel horrified or even to enjoy anything." Of the novella *Wise Blood:* "The book was not agin free-will . . . which all the characters had plenty of and exercised. . . . The thought is all Catholic, perhaps overbearingly so." The celebration of the Mass, the taking of the Eucharist (which Flannery believed to *be* Christ's actual body and blood, and not "merely" a symbol), were for Flannery the "center of existence"; "all the rest of life is expendable." Though Flannery's ill-health must have caused her untold suffering, she insists upon the fact that such suffering, coming from personal *experience,* is less significant than the Church's teachings. If one gains in insight it is primarily through the Church: "simply from listening to what the Church teaches." God is Love, and all good, all complete, all powerful. That children may suffer hideous deaths is of course a mystery, not to be comprehended by mortal man, but there is never any doubt that God is All Good. Flannery, unlike her marvelous comic creation Hulga (who believes defiantly in nothing, and has a wooden leg), *believes* and *accepts* witout the faintest protest.

The piety is touching, if sometimes implausible, and certainly it tells us nothing about the art to which Flannery devoted herself. The conservatism is rather more unpleasant, suggesting, as conservatism so frequently does, a refusal to examine one's beliefs, even one's vocabulary. I was saddened to read, and could not help interpreting in the context of the speaker's debilitating illness, and the small likelihood of *her* ever conceiving an unwanted child, such remarks as these:

> The Church's stand on birth control is the most absolutely spiritual of all her stands and with all of us being materialists at heart, there is little wonder that it causes unease. I wish various (priests) would quit trying to defend it by saying that the world can support 40 billion. I will rejoice in the day when they say: This is right, whether we all rot on top of each other or not, dear children. . . . Either practice restraint or be prepared for crowding. . . . (June 1959)

By twisting words about Flannery can convince herself that the Church's stand on birth control is "liberal"! Though she is well aware of the Church's history of persecution, she nevertheless insists in an ongoing debate with one of her closest friends, "A," that one cannot connect the Church with a belief in the use of force. "The Church is a mystical body which cannot, does not, believe in the use of force (in the sense of forcing conscience, denying the rights of conscience, etc.). I know all her hair-raising history . . . but principle must be separated from policy" (September 1955). In such circumspect, sophistic ways have the meek always aligned themselves with the bullies, allowing the organization, the hierarchy, to be their con-science for them, and to commit those crimes the meek would never dare entertain, even in fantasy. One has the feeling, in reading these passages, that the imaginative, artistic Flannery O'Connor had been nearly silenced by the bigot—and would have to take her revenge in art.

Though she had, evidently, no more than a conventional critical sensibility—she dismissed Randall Jarrell's marvelous *Pictures from an Institution* as bad fiction, she referred to Virginia Woolf as a "nut," and declared that she couldn't tell Mozart from Spike Jones, and despised the piano "and all its works"—she did possess a highly reliable talent for assessing her own work. She seems always to have known that she wrote well; that she *was* gifted. She saw how *Wise Blood* failed, she saw how certain of her stories—"Revelation," "Judgment Day," "Parker's Back"—succeeded beautifully. Having spent months on the long story, *The Lame Shall Enter First,* she saw that it simply didn't come off, and tried—too late, as it happened—to stop its publication in *Sewanee Review.* Her instincts about her own fiction were always right. She wrote ingenious parables of the spiritual life, and her characters were drawn with broad, slashing strokes—"I am not one of the subtle sensitive writers like Eudora Welty," she says—meant to suggest, but not to embody, "reality." A creator of romances, like Hawthorne, or even Poe; but one with a fine, sharp eye for the absurd. (It is not surprising that she first wanted to be a cartoonist, and sent off cartoons, week after week, to

The New Yorker, where they were invariably rejected.) Though she could not resist traveling to writers' conferences and to universities, where, in her words, "clichés are swapped" about the art of writing, she always knew that the process of creation was subjected to no rules, and that, as an artist, she "discovered" the truth of her stories in the writing of them. She enjoyed writing—perhaps it is not an exaggeration to say that she lived for it, and in it. Easily exhausted, she forced herself to work two or three hours every day, in the morning, and managed by this discipline to write about one story a year during the worst periods. During the final year of her life, 1964, when everything seemed to go wrong (tumor, operation, infections, reactivation of lupus, side effects of cortisone) she was completing the volume that would be her finest achievement, *Everything That Rises Must Converge,* which would be published, to wide critical acclaim, after her death. (One cannot imagine an ailing person less given to self-pity. When, as a fairly young woman, she learned that she would probably be on crutches the rest of her life, she says merely, "So, so much for that. I will henceforth be a structure with flying buttresses. . . ." Writing to a friend, Louise Abbot, in 1964, she says that she must submit to an operation because "I have a large tumor and if they don't make haste and get rid of it, they will have to remove me and leave it." It is only near the very end of her life that she says, briefly, to the same friend: "Prayers requested. I am sick of being sick.")

Partly because of her condition, and partly because of her temperament, Flannery O'Connor seems to have lived one of the most circumscribed lives ever lived by a distinguished artist. In a sense she enjoyed a prolonged childhood which was never ravaged by adolescence or the complications of "adult" life. (Judging by the collected letters and by Sally Fitzgerald's remarks, Flannery did not, evidently, write a single love letter, and there are no allusions to romantic relationships in her letters to friends. At the age of thirty-seven she writes defiantly to a friend, "I've usually had my own room but it's always been subject to intrusion. The only thing in mine that is not subject to intrusion is my desk. Nobody lays a hand on that, boy." Nobody meaning, of course, her mother Regina.)

"As for biographies," Flannery said in 1958, "there won't be any biographies of me because, for only one reason, lives spent between the house and the chicken yard do not make exciting copy." But we measure an artist by the quality and depth of interior vision, and by the maginitude of achievement: and by these standards Flannery O'Connor is one of our finest writers. *The Habit of Being* is a deeply moving, deeply disturbing, and ultimately very beautiful record of a highly complex woman artist whose art was, perhaps, too profound for even the critic in her to grasp.

Notes

Imaginary Cities: America

1. Saul Bellow, *Humboldt's Gift* (New York: Viking Press, 1975), p. 9.

2. Anzia Yezierska, "My Last Hollywood Script," in *The Open Cage: An Anzia Yezierska Collection* (New York: Persea Books, 1979), p. 187.

3. Saul Bellow, *Mr. Sammler's Planet* (New York: Viking Press, 1969), p. 26. Bellow's Sammler broods: "The many impressions and experiences of life seemed no longer to occur each in its own proper space, in sequence, each with its recognizable religious or aesthetic importance, but human beings suffered the humiliations of inconsequence, of confused styles, of a long life containing several separate lives. In fact the whole experience of mankind was now covering each separate life in its flood. . . . Compelling the frail person to receive, to register, depriving him because of volume, of mass, of the power to impart design."

4. Donald Barthelme, "City Life," in *City Life* (New York: Farrar, Straus & Giroux, 1970), p. 166.

5. Stephen Crane, *Maggie: A Girl of the Streets* (New York: Fawcett, 1978), pp. 26–28.

6. Theodore Dreiser, *Sister Carrie* (New York: Modern Library, 1925), p. 2.

7. *Ibid.*, p. 83.

8. Anzia Yezierska, *Bread Givers* (New York: Persea Books, 1979), p. 9.

9. *Ibid.*, p. 138.

10. *Ibid.*, p. 155.

11. *Ibid.*, p. 231.

12. Harriette Arnow is the author of a number of novels, but her masterpiece is *The Dollmaker,* first published in 1954 and reprinted by Avon Books in 1972. Since I wrote the Afterword for this edition I hesitate to repeat myself, except to emphasize the fact that *The Dollmaker,* set in Kentucky and Detroit during the closing months of World War II, is as significant a work as any by John Steinbeck and may bear comparison, in some respects at least, with the novels of William Faulkner.

13. William James, letter to Henry James, 1907; in F. O. Matthiessen, *The James Family* (New York: Vintage Books, 1980), p. 313.

14. Saul Bellow, *The Adventures of Augie March* (New York: Modern Library, 1965), p. 39. Originally published in 1953.

15. *Ibid.*, p. 124.

16. *Ibid.*, p. 62.

17. *Ibid.*, p. 90.

18. *Ibid.*, p. 330.

19. Saul Bellow, *Herzog* (New York: Viking Press, 1961), p. 333.

20. *Ibid.*, p. 317.

21. Saul Bellow, *Mr. Sammler's Planet* (New York: Viking Press, 1970), p. 89.

22. *Ibid.*, pp. 279–280.

23. *Humboldt's Gift,* p. 118.

24. *Ibid.*, p. 155.

25. "Self-Interview" by Saul Bellow in *The Ontario Review,* Fall-Winter 1975–76, pp. 51–60.

26. *Humboldt's Gift,* p. 115.

27. From *They Feed They Lion* (New York: Atheneum, 1972).

28. *The Collected Stories of Hortense Calisher* (New York: Arbor House, 1975), p. 502.

29. Donald Barthelme, "The Glass Mountain," in *City Life,* pp. 64–65.

30. Barthelme, "The Balloon," in *Unspeakable Practices, Unnatural Acts* (New York: Farrar, Straus & Giroux, 1968), p. 21.

31. Barthelme, "Brain Damage," in *City Life,* p. 146.

32. John Updike, "Gesturing," in *Too Far to Go* (New York: Fawcett, 1979), pp. 222–223.

"At Least I Have Made a Woman of Her"

1. Flaubert's strategy in many of his letters to his reproachful mistress Louise Colet was to keep the dissatisfied woman at a distance, in Paris. "You speak of your discouragements," he says in a letter of 1852. "If you could see mine! Sometimes I don't understand why my arms don't drop from my body with fatigue, why my brains don't melt away. I am leading a stern existence, stripped of all external pleasure. . . ."

2. Yeats develops this Shelleyesque sentiment at length in "The Symbolism of Poetry," from *Essays and Introductions* (New York: Macmillan, 1961). Originally published in 1900.

3. This representative hymn to "Woman's patriotism" was written by a popular lady poet, Mrs. L. H. Sigourney, in 1846. Quoted in the magazine *The Ladies' Wreath: Devoted to Literature, Industry, and Religion* (New York, 1847), p. 25.

4. Jennie Calder, *Women and Marriage in Victorian Fiction* (New York: Oxford University Press, 1976), p. 59.

5. John R. Reed, *Victorian Conventions* (Athens, Ohio: Ohio University Press, 1975), p. 52.

6. Ronald W. Clark, *Freud: The Man and the Cause* (New York: Random House, 1980), p. 45.

7. Reed, p. 57.

8. Beverly Voloshin, "A Historical Note on Women's Fiction: A Reply to Annette Kolodny," in *Critical Inquiry,* Summer 1976, p. 820.

9. Mrs. E. D. E. N. Southworth, *The Discarded Daughter; or The Children of the Isle* (New York, 1876), p. 183.

10. *Ibid.,* p. 26.

11. *Ibid.,* p. 163.

12. Joseph Conrad, *Nostromo* (New York: Modern Library, 1951), pp. 73–74. Originally published in 1904.

13. D. H. Lawrence, *Women in Love* (New York: Modern Library, 1950), p. 217.

14. Anthony Alpers, *The Life of Katherine Mansfield* (New York: Viking Press, 1980), pp. 310–311.

15. *Women in Love,* p. 530.

16. D. H. Lawrence, *Lady Chatterly's Lover* (New York: New American Library, 1962), pp. 189–191. Originally published in 1928.

17. D. H. Lawrence, *The Complete Stories,* vol. 2 (New York: Viking Press, 1964), p. 569.

18. William Faulkner, *Light in August* (New York: Modern Library, 1959), p. 222. Originally published 1932. This famous passage is often cited as an expression of Faulkner's sense of determinism, his fatalism, regarding white-black relations. One can, however, substitute *women* for *Negroes* in Faulkner's closed cosmology, in representative passages:

> I had seen and known Negroes since I could remember [says Johanna Burden]. I just looked at them as I did at rain, or furniture, or food . . . But after that I seemed to see them for the first time not as people, but as a thing, a shadow in which I lived, we lived, all white people, all other people. I thought of all the children coming forever and ever into the world, white, with the black shadow already falling upon them before they drew breath. And I seemed to see the black shadow in the shape of a cross. And it seemed like the white babies were struggling, even before they drew breath, to escape from the shadow that was not only upon them but beneath them too, flung out like their arms were flung out, as if they were nailed to the cross. (p. 221)

19. Faulkner's tall tale shades into forthright Surrealism—or "magic realism," as critical jargon would have it—in Gabriel García Marquez's

portrait of the irresistible Remedios the Beauty, a Eula-inspired female who eventually ascends to heaven in *One Hundred Years of Solitude* (New York: Harper & Row, 1970).

20. *Light in August,* p. 206.

21. Temple Drake, the judge's daughter, is seventeen years old at the time of her abduction by Popeye, neither a child nor a woman yet readily corrupted: despite her ill-treatment by men she soon becomes a nymphomaniac:

"She felt long shuddering waves of physical desire going over her, draining the color from her mouth, drawing her eyeballs back into her skull in a shuddering swoon. . . . When he touched her she sprang like a bow, hurling herself upon him, her mouth gaped and ugly like that of a dying fish as she writhed her loins against him."

Temple Drake is still "virginal," however; indeed, impenetrable. *Sanctuary* makes the explicit statement that chaste Southern womanhood and besotted nymphomania, verging on outright madness, are very nearly identical. (*Sanctuary* was published in 1932.)

The Magnanimity of Wuthering Heights

1. Emily Bronte, *Wuthering Heights* (New York: Modern Library, n.d.), p. 94.

2. *Ibid.,* p. 194.

3. *Ibid.,* p. 374.

4. *Ibid.,* p. 375.

5. *Ibid.,* p. 145.

6. Sylvia Plath, "Wuthering Heights," from *Crossing the Water* (New York: Harper & Row, 1971).

7. *Wuthering Heights,* pp. 174–175.

8. *Ibid.,* p. 176.

9. *Ibid.,* p. 331.

10. *Ibid.,* p. 56.

11. *Ibid.,* p. 296.

12. *Ibid.,* p. 339.

13. *Ibid.,* p. 62.

Charles Dodgson's Golden Hours

1. Rogert Lancelyn Green, "Alice," in *Aspects of Alice,* edited by Robert Phillips (New York: Vanguard Press, 1971).

2. Martin Gardner's Introduction, *The Hunting of the Snark* (Los Altos, California: William Kaufmann, Inc., 1981).

3. Alice alone of Wonderland's inhabitants insists upon the need for rules, answers, conclusions, ways of behaving, ends. She brings a pristine "rationalist's" expectations to a thoroughly irrational world: it is she who hopes for a conclusion to the Mouse's pitiable tale, she who complains that the croquet players don't "play at all fairly." Alice's resistance to the counterlogic of Wonderland makes her both a comic and a sympathetic figure, and a recognizable "heroine."

4. A small controversy has arisen over the Beaver's precise sex: *he, she,* and *it* have been variously proposed. See Gardner's amusing footnote, p. 51 of the 1981 edition.

5. "A Commentary on the *Snark,*" by Snarkophilus Snobbs. An almost too prodigious parody of Snark-hunting, symbol-hunting, and the predicament of "Humanity in search of the Absolute." For Lewis Carroll, like Falstaff, is not only witty in himself but the cause of wit—albeit often a rather strained wit—in others.

John Updike's American Comedies

1. *Museums and Women* (New York: Fawcett, 1972), p. 20.

2. *Couples* (New York: Alfred A. Knopf, 1968), epigraph, p. v.

3. *Bech: A Book* (New York: Alfred A. Knopf, 1970), p. 187.

4. When someone denounced Gothic architecture as a fussy multiplication of accents that demonstrated only "a belief in the virtue of *quantity,*" James Joyce stated that he did something similar in words; there was no need to force the trivial into a symbolic expression of "beauty" since it is

already, by simply existing, beautiful. The emotional and artistic consequences of such a belief, however admirable the belief, are sometimes dangerous: the writer finds himself unable to stop the multiplication of specific detail. There is a scholastic maxim *(omnis determinatio est negatio)* that, in psychological terms, warns against the generous dissolving of the ego in its submission to all that is outside it. What some critics dislike in Updike is this tendency toward detail for its own sake, as in *Couples* at the start of a dramatic scene one is sometimes given the setting at too great a length, or in *Rabbit Redux* one is dizzily informed of the furnishings of the Angstroms' house while scandalous events are taking place. The "external circumstances" of the visual world can be an exhausting burden. One example (p. 175) from *The Centaur:* "Vera enters the back of the auditorium by one of the broad doors that are propped open on little rubber-footed legs which unhinge at a kick from snug brass fittings." This naturalism, this fidelity to the concreteness of things, shades into the "absurdistic" techniques of Céline, Beckett, Robbe-Grillet, Ionesco, and many others, as faith in the divinity of things as things is lost.

5. *The Centaur* (New York: Alfred A. Knopf, 1963) and *Of the Farm* (New York: Alfred A. Knopf, 1966) illuminate one another, just as, scattered in his fiction but always recognizable as *the* nuclear fable of Updike's life, a certain set of tensions appears and reappears. At the center is the mother who waits out in Nature, patient, diabolically clever, more than a match for any female rival who would tempt her son away from her, and more than a match for the son himself. Hence the rudeness, the bluntness, the devastating accuracy of Mrs. Robinson of *Of the Farm,* who, when her thirty-five-year-old son challenges her by saying (p. 35), "You can't reduce everything to money," replies at once: "What would you reduce it to? Sex?" She knows him completely, from the inside, and the means by which Joey is able to transcend his situation—his mortality—is belittled simply by being named.

6. *The Centaur,* pp. 205–206.

7. *Ibid.,* p. 178.

8. *Bech: A Book,* p. 115. Twelve years later, in the sequel *Bech Is Back,* Bech's long-awaited novel *Think Big* has at last been published—and, to its author's amazement, becomes a best-seller. So his "preening, lovemaking, and typing" have, after all, yielded fruit of a sort; though, by this weary time in his career, poor Bech has not only married but has been divorced; and, when last seen, finds himself cast upon the flotsam of a

New York publishing world as terrifying in its emptiness as anything envisioned during his panic. "Radiant America; where else but here? Still, Bech, sifting the gathering with his inspired gaze, was not quite satisfied. Another word occurred to him. *Treyf,* he thought. Unclean." (*Bech Is Back,* p. 195.)

9. A dozen years later, in another celebrated sequel, Rabbit Angstrom discovers himself adrift in a surprisingly serene middle age, in which domestic problems present themselves with the frequency (and the texture) of situation-comedy complications. Yet, for all Rabbit's problems, he *is* rich, at least in a manner of speaking; and convinced that life is sweet, though finite. Or is it sweet because finite? At the conclusion of *Rabbit Is Rich* he holds his son's baby in his lap and muses: "Through all this she has pushed to be here, in his lap, his hands, a real presence hardly weighing anything, but alive. Fortune's hostage, heart's desire, a granddaughter. His. Another nail in his coffin. His."

10. Another of Updike's several undeveloped shadow-selves is that of a distinctly American theologian, as his thoughtful essays on Barth, Tillich, and de Rougemont (in *Assorted Prose,* 1965) and such stories as "The Astronomer" (in *Pigeon Feathers,* 1962) make clear.

11. *Couples,* p. 429.

12. *The Centaur,* p. 221.

13. *Ibid.,* p. 189.